“This book is greatly needed at a profound vision of the Sufi tradition has been marginalised in much Islamic discourse. Sufi’s have consistently emphasised the crucial fact that mercy and compassion lie at the heart of the religious quest and this message is vitally important in our dangerously polarised world.”

Karen Armstrong, author of best selling books, *Muhammad: A Prophet for our time*, *Islam: A Short History*, *A History of God* and *Fields of Blood*.

“Terrorist attacks by militant extremists like Al Qaeda and ISIS and the exponential growth of Islamophobia by well funded organizations have brush-stroked the faith of the vast majority of mainstream Muslims. *Islam: The Faith of Love and Happiness* offers an antidote, to foster a paradigm shift to counter this dark view of Islam by presenting the heart of Islam, the extent to which Islam, the Quran and Muhammad offer a message of love and happiness.”

John L. Esposito, Professor of Islamic Studies, Georgetown University.

“This practical book presents the inner depths of Sufi teachings in a way that is directly relevant to our constant efforts to reach for happiness.”

Prof Komaruddin Hidayat, Islamic scholar and bestselling author of *Life’s Journey*

Islam

The Faith of Love and Happiness

Haidar Bagir

KUBE PUBLISHING

Islam: The Faith of Love and Happiness

Published by
Kube Publishing Ltd
Markfield Conference Centre
Ratby Lane, Markfield,
Leicestershire LE67 9SY
United Kingdom
Tel: +44 (0)1530 249230 Fax: +44 (0)1530 249656
Email: info@kubepublishing.com
Website: www.kubepublishing.com

English edition exclusively published and distributed by Kube Publishing Ltd 2017 CE/1438 AH

Cataloguing-in-Publication Data is available from the British Library

ISBN: 978-1-84774-110-3 *paperback*

Cover/Book design & Layout Nasir Cadir
Printed by: Akcent Media - UK

Dedication

This little book is dedicated to my children—
Muhammad Irfan, Mustafa Kamil, Ali Riza and
Syarifa Rahima, in the hope that Allah bestows
you all with sincere love for Allah, family, friends,
fellow humans and all elements of the universe.

...They (the *Anṣār*) love those who have migrated to them (the *Muhājirūn*) and do not covet what has been given them; they even prefer them above themselves though poverty be their own lot. And whosoever are preserved from their own greed, such are the ones that shall attain to a happy state! (*mufliḥūn*). (*al-Ḥashr* 59: 9)

Contents

Part III
Sources of Happiness

Preface

LOOKING BACK, I cannot recall a time when I was not interested in the issue of love in religion. As for happiness, although my sentimental temperament has always been concerned with it, this intensified when I experienced symptoms of depression for the first time. Yes, indeed, I went through that experience. Although, I suspect that the symptoms were more related to biological or hormonal factors.

At that time I had just passed my half-century, so understandably, I suppose, it was a phenomenon commonly called the andropause. Although my life—like any other man's life—was not entirely without problems, I felt that God had given me so many blessings. I have felt quite happy throughout my life, being raised in a loving family and raising my own family today. Thank God, I am also typically unflustered in the face of problems.

However, the symptoms of depression were still symptoms that had to be overcome. I had refused to see a doctor and take any mood-restoring medication. I felt, as long as I was able to tackle the problems, I would try to find other ways to solve them, and these symptoms would disappear by themselves. And, thank God, that's exactly what happened. I tried to keep going back to God each time the uncomfortable depressive feelings came knocking–there were times when such feelings attacked rather frequently. I tried to assuage my spiritual restlessness by redoubling my efforts to find answers to various unresolved transcendental issues. Aside from that, I tried tirelessly to seek meanings that I could give to my life, since depressive symptoms would always somehow involve the lack of meaning in life. I suppose I need to briefly say here that my life, which was relatively smooth, has perhaps played a role in the origin of my depression, because–at one point–I felt I was losing excitement in life. I have, more or less, achieved everything I ever expected in life, so what else would I need to pursue?

Due to my sentimental temperament, I tend to have empathy towards others–not only for those in need, but even for the well-to-do–who live a materially prosperous life in the cities but seem to lack meaning in their lives. Even on those few occasions when I had the opportunity to stay in the USA, I felt there were a lot of people who looked prosperous but were actually losing their vigour since there was not enough meaning in their lives. From quite early on in life, I have been keen to help people, within my own limitations, to overcome their suffering and misery, as well as in their search for meaning in life.

I think my religious and academic interest in a kind of Islamic mysticism–Sufism–has also largely contributed here, which may be a consequence of my sentimental temperament. Seeking answers for my spiritual restlessness, I found that the main concern of Sufism is indeed to address the question of spiritual thirst: the meaning of life. What is life? Where is it from? Where is it heading? In addition to this, if studied properly, Sufism is a spiritual understanding of religion based on relationships of reciprocal love between man and God, between man and his fellow men, as well as between man and the entire universe.

The more I learned and existentially internalized the teachings, the more convinced I became that Sufism is the remedy for the human problems of our times. Aside from addressing spiritual problems, it also deals with the lengthy conflicts that plague mankind. The problem of intolerance in all fields, the tendency towards an increasingly dominant selfishness, and the frail bond of human brotherhood.

Then, gradually, the issues of happiness and love began to dominate the various discourses that I conveyed throughout my daily life, to the extent that, upon hearing me speak at a national conference, a foreign observer said that my speech was like that of a pastor preaching a sermon.

Finally, in 2008, I was interviewed by *Kompas Daily*. In the interview I spoke about the importance of a paradigm shift in the religious understanding of Islam from a law-oriented religion to a love-oriented one. Because, as argued by phenomenologists of religion, including Gerard van der Leeuw, Islam is in fact no less than Christianity in its orientation towards love. This is confirmed by Annemarie Schimmel, who identifies the evidence to this effect from the works of Sufis throughout the history of Islamic thought. I see that these inaccuracies in understanding the paradigm affect not only those outside Islam, but also Muslims themselves. Only through this paradigm shift will Islam be able to show its real face as 'a mercy to the worlds', as opposed to the current reality in which Islam is mainly being portrayed as an exclusively political religion, sometimes even a violent one. (Of course I am also aware that such an image of Islam is partly shaped by both misunderstandings and misrepresentations on the part of some international media, especially the Western media.)

This book is the result of my reflections on two matters—love and happiness. Originally, there were two separate collections of writings that I later combined due to the similarity of their subject matter. Six chapters in the 'Introduction' try to explain both of these, while examining the relationship between the two. And, since this book tries to link love with happiness, the discussion in the 'Happiness' section is limited to topics of love for and contentment with Allah, and love for one's fellow human beings as the source of that happiness. I have also added substantial content, revised and rearranged the work to help the book read well in its current form.

I deliberately cite poignant stories at the beginning of each section to warm the heart, add to the spiritual impact, as well as to pave the way for a pleasant and readable prelude to the subject matter.. I have also incorporated extracts from the original writings of some philosophers and Sufis, and I hope this simple book will help readers to reflect further on the meaning of their lives, and also become a guide along our path to achieve the true happiness that we all desire.

I hope that aside from being an accessible non-academic work, this book can give an idea to the reader that Islam is genuinely a love-oriented religion. Moreover, the law-oriented part of our religion, although no less important, should be placed in the context of the *love* orientation which is rooted in the heart of this religion.

Finally, I would like to thank the Mizan Group for publishing most of my writings in this book; Lite FM, that has for several years given me the opportunity to explore these issues in a programme broadcast every Friday morning (*Lite is Beautiful*); Pak Cecep Romli, who helped me with the editing and adding the words of wisdom; the staff of Noura Books, who helped me with the trifles of pre-printing; Sayed Hyder for editing and retranslating this book into English, as well as providing very valuable input, and again Mizan Publishers, who were willing to publish the original Indonesian version of this book.

May Allah register this modest work as a good deed on my way towards His pleasure.

Haidar Bagir

Part I

Dive into Love, Seize Happiness

I

Happiness as the Highest Goal

HAPPINESS (*SA'ĀDAH)* REPRESENTS the highest goal of mankind during their tenure here in this world. It can be reasoned that happiness is the main concern of everyone on earth. Indeed, every human endeavour is intended to assist in obtaining happiness. This appears in numerous verses of the Qur'an which place the joy of life – both in this world and in the afterlife – as the purpose of human existence (creation):

> *Whoever behaves righteously, whether male or female, while they are a believer, We will surely cause them to live a good life, and We will surely give them a reward better than what they do.* (*al-Naḥl* 16: 97)

Ibn 'Abbas, the main *mufassir* (exegete) among the Companions of the Prophet (peace be upon him), interprets the phrase 'a good life' (*ḥayāh ṭayyibah*) as happiness (in this world). Indeed, if we humans follow rather than violate our nature, we are truly created for happiness (*falāḥ*):

> *And by the soul and by Him Who perfectly proportioned it, and imbued it with (the consciousness of) its evil and its piety: He who purifies it will prosper/be happy (aflaḥa), and he who suppresses it will be ruined.* (*al-Shams* 91: 7–10)

The problem is that there is a mistaken perception amongst some people in Muslim societies that if we want to be happy in the Hereafter, we have to live miserably in the world. Sometimes this belief stems from a hadith of the Prophet (peace be upon him) which states that life is a prison for the believer, while it is heaven for unbelievers. Or part of another hadith which states that people who laugh much in this world will end up crying a lot in the Hereafter. So do not be surprised if there are some people who think that people of strong faith/creed must maintain a grim or melancholic disposition. Is this belief really sound?

A good example of how a faithful Muslim leads his life, and lives in this world with serenity, is in the life of Ḥasan b. ʿAlī b. Abī Ṭālib, the grandson of the Prophet (peace be upon him). He was known to have a neat and clean appearance, well-groomed and elegant, in short, very pleasing to the eye. So much so that his attire became a source of vilification by those who detested him.

Once a disbeliever who despised Ḥasan b. ʿAlī intercepted him and said: 'Your grandfather (Prophet Muhammad) had said, the world is a prison for a believer. And yet you live in it with so much ease.'

Ḥasan b. ʿAlī responded: 'My life, although good and enjoyable in this world, when compared to the joy and happiness that I will get in the Hereafter, is like Hell. Imagine the pleasure I would obtain if I enter His Heaven? While your life is hard in this world, and will be harder still in the Hereafter.'

While at the same time, according to the *āyah* (16:97) above, those who are pious and faithful, will be awarded a far better life of happiness as compared to what they were already given in this world.

Ḥasan b. 'Alī's outlook and deportment can thus be understood in the context of the aforementioned *āyah*. According to him, happiness in this world is at a far lower relative level when compared to life in the Hereafter, resulting in what the Prophet (peace be upon him) said: it may aptly be compared to the life of a prisoner.

There is another interesting *āyah* concerning how a believer leads a life full of happiness in this world:

> *[O Prophet], announce glad tidings to those who believe and do righteous deeds , that for them are gardens beneath which rivers flow. Their fruits will have such resemblance to those of the earth that whenever they will be provided with those fruits they will say: 'It was this that was granted to us on earth before.' For them there shall be pure spouses, and there they shall abide forever.* (*al-Baqarah* 2: 25)

It is important to draw our attention to the expression used by the inhabitants of Paradise, 'It was this that was granted to us on earth before.' Indirectly, this verse is implying that someone who would go to Heaven would have already tasted the pleasures of Paradise while they were in this world. The people of Paradise will find that whatever they receive or experience, they would have – to a certain extent – received and experienced while they were in the world.

Again, in conclusion, those who are of the faith and do good deeds are not only guaranteed by Allah to be among those upon whom happiness is conferred in the Hereafter, but also in this world. This is how a Muslim should approach life, by appreciating the sources of happiness in it; in other words, we should live a life of happiness in this world in order to reach a far higher level of happiness in the afterlife. Exactly as mentioned in His statement:

> *Seek, by means of the wealth that Allah has granted you, the Abode of the Hereafter, but forget not your share in this world!* (*al-Qaṣaṣ* 28: 77)

2

What is Happiness?

IT IS DOUBTFUL that anyone would disagree that the purpose of his or her life on this earth is to achieve happiness (*sa'ādah*). Although happiness may be understood differently by different people–as psychological, intellectual or spiritual–all agree with regards to its nature. It is happiness that makes humans passionate, excited and full of life, while encouraging us to spread tranquillity, peace, meaningfulness and fulfilment. Meanwhile, the opposite of happiness, i.e. misery (*shaqāwah*) is in the same league as anxiety, chaos and a life devoid of meaning.

Happiness in the Islamic tradition is referred to as *surūr*, *faraḥ* (joy) and, more fundamentally, *sa'ādah*, *ṭīb* and *falāḥ*.[1] It must be emphasized that happiness is not the

1. *Sa'adah* means 'happiness' or 'success'. While the word *tib* is derived from the same word as *tayyibah*, which means 'blissful'; see Qur'an, *al-Nahl* 16: 97, and the explanation below. For an enlightening discussion of the meaning of *falah* as happiness, see Jalaluddin Rakhmat's *Reaching Happiness*, published by Simbiosa Rekatama Media, 2009, pp. 24–27.

same as an assortment of pleasures. It is perfectly possible for one to lead a life of pleasures, without being happy. Happiness also does not mean the absence of hardship or suffering. This is because suffering may come and go, but they do not undermine the existence of happiness. This is what is referred to as *underlying happiness* (happiness that always exists in our lives).

Nor is happiness the same as ephemeral moments of pleasure. Such moments come without any assurance that they may not be immediately succeeded by a feeling of emptiness; nor are such moments free from anxiety about the prospect of a void after the pleasure is gone. Therefore, such pleasure never really takes root in the depths of the heart. Rather, it is more akin to something perfunctory floating on the surface of the superficiality of our lives.

Seen and felt through the foundation of underlying happiness, whatever happens on the surface of our lives will penetrate the heart as an entity that brings us positive meaning, reassuring us and bringing us happiness. It is possible that we may be struck with adversity and grief, but having the belief that everything in our life is essentially good, positive and for our well-being, will help us remain undaunted. Happiness gives a more enduring vision of peace and tranquillity. This is why some people identify happiness with 'enduring virtues' (*al-bāqiyāt al-ṣāliḥāt*) as revealed by Him:

> *Wealth and children are an adornment of the life of the world. But the enduring virtues are the best in the sight of your Lord in reward, and far better a source of hope.* (*al-Kahf* 18: 46)

Al-bāqiyāt al-ṣāliḥāt are nothing but good deeds that one does for the good of others, often at the cost of sacrificing our own interest(s), providing a strong foundation for a sustainable and enduring underlying happiness.

Indeed, happiness is neither physical nor psychological–if *psyche* is understood superficially to be merely the collective indicators of cerebral-consciousness. Happiness is profoundly spiritual in nature–not necessarily of the ritual kind–but rather that associated with the heart. Spirituality is the force within humans that is not only superior to the cerebral intellectual faculty, but also surpasses emotions and feelings which–despite being linked to the heart–have yet to overcome their preliminary instability and imbalance. Indeed, emotions and feelings have all the ingredients to be stable and bring peace, tranquillity and happiness, but the combination does not always occur in suitable proportions.

When these emotions are stable, no occurrence outside of our hearts can disturb the state of balance that has been achieved, which is this underlying happiness. There would be no joy so unrestrained as to backfire, opening the possibility of subsequent misery, nor any sorrow so immense that would shatter the foundation of our happiness. Nor would any events in our transient life have so deep an effect as to upset our happiness. Just as a rock flung into shallow waters produces large ripples but in the deep ocean the same rock will hardly disturb its tranquil surface.

Indeed, happiness is intrinsic–residing in our hearts–not extrinsic or dependent on the fleeting occurrences in our daily lives. For those who have achieved this underlying happiness, anything can happen in one's 'external' life, while the state of happiness remains stable. For those who have it, comfort and adversity are relative and neither have their own independent meaning. Relative to the underlying happiness, there is no adversity. Once placed on the foundation of this happiness, everything becomes a cause of happiness. Pleasure and pain become limited to outward appearances—or packaging. In reality, they are invariably meant to bring happiness. This is what makes many people state: at its heart happiness (and misery) is a product of perception. If we perceive anything positively, it will contribute to our happiness, though its outer appearance or packaging may look like hardship. Conversely, if we perceive anything negatively, it can give birth to misery, despite its beautiful outer appearance or packaging.

On top of that, we can say that sadness is something that is truly necessary in order to identify and feel happiness. People who have never felt sorrow or worry would be immune or desensitized towards happiness. A simple inconvenience can be the basis on which we can truly feel and appreciate happiness. *Sayyidunā* ʿAlī, *karram Allāh wajhah* (may Allah ennoble his countenance), once stated: 'A person will not feel the sweetness of happiness (*saʿādah*), till he tastes the bitterness of grief (*shaqāwah*).' It may be appropriate to note that, although the word *shaqāwah* is often regarded as the opposite of *saʿādah* and of other words that express happiness, *shaqāwah*, unlike *saʿādah*, should never be understood as having the possibility of perpetuity. God's affection is so infinite that it closes all possibilities for perpetual *shaqāwah* or eternal misery. However, *shaqāwah* is always seen as the precursor to *sa'ādah*. In other words, *sa'ādah* is the principle of human life, while *shaqāwah* is an exception, *shaqāwah* is required merely as a yardstick, through which one can identify and appreciate happiness. At the very least, *shaqāwah* can be seen as God's means of instructing and guiding us so that we are driven to be better.

3

Happiness is a Matter of Meaning

NO ONE WOULD contend that living in this world is related to physical and material wellbeing. For God has given man a corporeal mantle such that if he chooses to engage the physical aspects alone, he can only achieve physical survival. Furthermore, it is also hard not to agree that at its pinnacle, happiness is spiritual. Indeed, happiness is not mere sensuous pleasure, but rather tranquillity and contentment. Therefore, it can be reasonably said that happiness cannot be achieved by merely satisfying our physical needs. Why? Because there are considerably more spiritual needs to fulfil, that have nothing to do with our physical needs. In fact our spiritual or psychological needs are not always in accordance with our physical wants and needs, at times even being antithetical. For example, in the case of needing to love, we actually gain (spiritual) happiness only by providing for the people we love, rather than by demanding and taking from them for our own egoistic satisfaction. Even if there is a physical relationship, the nourishment for our soul and spirit comes from the meanings extracted from the fulfilment of our physical needs rather than from the physical needs themselves. Indeed, as regards both physical and spiritual needs, human happiness is associated with the creation of meaning in our lives, which is in line with our spiritual needs, as opposed to such concrete activities by themselves.

As an illustration, our physical, and perhaps also our (lower) psychological needs and wants demand a certain level of so-called (worldly) success. Quite a few people, unfortunately, confuse worldly success with happiness. Happiness is undoubtedly related to success. However, not many people realize that success does not guarantee happiness. On the contrary, it is happiness, as we shall see, that guarantees success.

Success is usually defined as the attainment of wealth, position, honour and the like, and is accorded synonyms such as 'accomplishment', 'prosperity' and 'fame'. For some people, happiness is even seen as one of the two sides of a coin, the other being success. Now, is it correct to say that being happy is a natural psychological outcome of achieving success?

In actual fact, success can result in unhappiness. Experts, such as Paul Pearsall[1] refer to this kind of success as 'bitter success', i.e. success that only gives birth to misery in the one experiencing success. How many successful people get trapped in a veritable state of anxiety even after they might feel that they have achieved success? Even worse is experiencing the so called 'hedonic treadmill' in which – after reaching a certain level of

---

1. Paul Pearsall, *Toxic Success: How to Stop Striving and Start Thriving*, Inner Ocean Publishing, Hawaii, 2002.

success in the form of possession of a certain amount of wealth – everything does not add up to our happiness and might lead one to suffer from a deep depression.

Pursuing success for its own sake can only result in a feeling of emptiness, caused by the loss of excitement that had hitherto existed in the pursuit of success, as soon as it is achieved. Furthermore, if out of desperation, one extends the goal further, and again succeeds in achieving the new goal, it will, in turn, only make the situation worse, by enhancing the feeling of emptiness even as the new goal is achieved. Setting new goals to be achieved in the desire to find happiness yet to be found in prior success, is exactly like chasing a mirage, always out of reach, which recedes as we are deluded into thinking that we are near. Or like a horse chasing the proverbial carrot, dangling in front, not realizing that it will always be beyond reach.

How many such people, then, contemplate ending their lives, and even end up going through with it even though they are at the peak of their success? And how many more seek to escape into a drug- or alcohol-induced stupor?

Indeed, success only contributes to happiness when one has developed a sound understanding of the meaning of success, and happiness too. Now, it is time to find out the secret of making success the source of our happiness.

It is actually quite simple: imbue your success with meaning, thereby making it meaningful success. The bigger, and the more inexhaustible the meaning, the more it guarantees happiness – and a lasting one at that.

What are we referring to when we use the term 'meaning'?

Meaning is the psychological impact of a situation or event on one's experiences. In this context, meaning is understood in its positive connotation, that is, as something that generates positive emotions. Barbara Frederickson identifies the ten most common positive emotions as joy, gratitude, serenity, interest, hope, pride, amusement, inspiration, awe and love.

Put in other words, giving meaning to life is the prerequisite of true happiness. Indeed, happiness is no more and no less than a matter of the presence or absence of meaning in whatever we do in our lives. So, we should continue to strive to supply our lives with meaning, and spare them from desolation. Our true happiness is at stake here. As long as we have the will, we won't reach an impasse. The life we live, as God's creation, is never depleted of wisdom or positive meaning. Anything that happens, no matter how bad it looks at first, can certainly be rendered meaningful by those who maintain a positive outlook on life. Such people have a greater chance of happiness, while those who tend to be negative and cynical, in fact, plunge themselves into a self-created misery.

As shown by Martin Seligman[2], the most inexhaustible meaning one can imbue any endeavour with is altruism – the emotion felt when a person selflessly helps others, when they share the products of what they have successfully achieved with fellow human beings. As further shown by Seligman, 'the exercise of kindness is

2. Martin Seligman, *Authentic Happiness: Using the New Positive Psychology to Realize Your Potential for Lasting Fulfillment*. New York: Free Press, 2002, p. 9.

a *gratification*, in contrast to a pleasure.' Gratifying in the sense of lasting satisfaction and a feeling of harmony with one's inner nature. Indeed, not only can this meaning never be exhausted, it serves as the only thing that can really fulfil our primordial desire as compassionate and generous creatures of God, the Most Beneficent, the Most Compassionate. Actually, the concept of happiness is strongly associated with love and affection. Hence creating contentment and relief are the two greatest meanings of any worldly endeavour. After all, are we not in some sense 'theophanic' creatures, coming into being through the breath of His Spirit?

> *After I have created him and breathed into him of My spirit, fall you down, prostrating yourselves to him.* (*Ṣād* 38: 72)

A God, Whose nature is love, beneficence and compassion. Indeed, as creatures that have come into being as a consequence of God's breathing of His Spirit into Adam, the human being is compassionate in his primordial nature. No prospect of happiness is possible for him, except by fully realizing this spirit of compassion through concrete acts congruent with this nature. Yes, human happiness can only be realized through doing good and performing selfless deeds – through being loving and kind to one's fellow creatures, especially those in need.

...They (the Anṣār) love those who have migrated to them (the Muhājirūn) and do not covet what has been given them; they even prefer them above themselves though poverty be their own lot. And whosoever are preserved from their own greed, such are the ones that shall attain to a happy state! (mufliḥūn). (*al-Ḥashr* 59: 9)

4

Doing What is Beautiful (*Iḥsān*)

ONE DAY WHILE we were sitting with the Messenger of Allah (peace be upon him), there appeared before us a man dressed in extremely white clothes and with very black hair. No traces of travel were visible on him, and none of us knew him. He sat down before the Prophet (peace be upon him), rested his knees against his knees and placed his palms on his thighs, and said, 'O Muhammad! Inform me about Islam.' The Prophet (peace be upon him) said, 'Islam is that you should testify that there is no deity save Allah and that Muhammad is His Messenger, that you should perform *ṣalāh* (ritual prayer), pay the zakat (alms), fast during Ramadan, and perform hajj (pilgrimage) to the House (the Kaʿbah at Makkah), if you can find a way to it (or find the means for making the journey to it).' The man replied, 'You have spoken truly.' We were astonished at his thus questioning him and yet affirming that he was right. Then he went on to say, 'Inform me about *īmān* (faith).' He (the Messenger of Allah) answered, 'It is that you believe in Allah and His angels and His Books and His Messengers and in the Last Day, and in fate (*qadar*), both in its good and in its evil aspects.' He said, 'You have spoken truthfully.' Then he (the man) said, 'Inform me about *Iḥsān*.' He (the Messenger of Allah) answered, 'It is that you should serve Allah as though you could see Him, for though you cannot see Him yet He sees you'. ... Thereupon the man went off. I waited a while, and then he (the Messenger of Allah) said, 'O 'Umar, do you know who that questioner was?' I replied, 'Allah and His Messenger know best.' He said, 'That was Gabriel. He came to teach you your religion.'[1]

The word *iḥsān* is derived from *ḥusn*, which designates the quality of being good and beautiful. According to the lexicons, it means every positive quality (goodness, goodliness, beauty, comeliness, pleasantness, harmony, symmetry, desirability). The Qur'an employs the word *ḥasanah* (pl. *ḥasanāt*), twenty-nine times, from the same root as *ḥusn*, occurring six times, to mean a good or beautiful deed or thing. The Qur'an also uses the word *ḥusnā* as a noun meaning 'the best', 'the most beautiful' and 'desirable'. The word *iḥsān* is a means to do or to establish what is good and beautiful. The Qur'an uses the word and its active particle *muḥsin* (one who does what is beautiful) in seventy verses: 'Those who do what is beautiful [good] will receive the most beautiful and much more [than that]' (*Yunus* 10:26) and 'Indeed, unto God belongs all that is in the heavens and all that is on earth: and so He will reward those who do evil in accordance with what they did, and will reward those who do what is beautiful [good] with the most beautiful'

1. Narrated by Muslim.

(*al-Najm* 53:31). When we perform a deed as an act of worship, as if we see God while doing it or with the belief that God sees us, it is impossible that we won't do our utmost for our deed to be perfect. Let alone if it is driven by *īmān*, an intense love of God. As God Himself says in the Qur'an (*al-Baqarah* 2:165): 'Those who have attained to faith love God intensely, more than all else.'

God himself is designated as the one who does what is beautiful, as *al-Muḥsin* is one of the divine names. God's beautiful work began with the act of creation itself, in which the creation of the human being is done in the most beautiful form:

> *Such is He who knows all that is beyond the reach of a created being's perception, as well as all that can be witnessed by a creature's senses or mind: the Almighty, the Dispenser of Grace. Who makes most beautiful everything that He creates. Thus, He begins the creation of man out of clay then He causes him to be begotten out of the essence of a humble fluid; and then He forms him in accordance with what he is meant to be, and breathes into him of His spirit ...* (*al-Sajdah* 32: 6-9)

> *It is God who has made the earth a resting- place for you and the sky a canopy, and has formed you – and formed you so beautifully and provided for you sustenance out of the good things of life....* (*Ghāfir* 40: 64)

> *He has created the heavens and the earth in accordance with [an inner] reality, and has*

> *formed you – and formed you so beautifully, and with Him is your journey's end* ... (*al-Taghābun* 64: 3)

Since God does what is beautiful through creating human beings, human beings have the obligation to do what is beautiful in their relationships with God and other creatures: 'Do what is beautiful [unto others], as God has done what is beautiful to you.' (*al-Qaṣaṣ* 28: 77)

In a hadith, the Prophet (peace be upon him) taught us: 'God has prescribed doing what is beautiful for everything. (Even) when you kill, do the killing beautifully, and when you sacrifice, do the slaughtering beautifully. You should sharpen your blade so that the sacrificial animal does not suffer.'

In practice, *iḥsān* is doing good to fellow creatures in the most beautiful or most perfect manner: 'And worship God [alone], and do not ascribe divinity, in any way, to aught beside Him. And do the most beautiful good unto your parents, and near of kin, and unto orphans, and the needy, and the neighbour from among your own people, and the neighbour who is a stranger, and the friend by your side, and the wayfarer, and those whom you rightfully possess. Verily, God does not love any of those who, full of self-conceit, act in a boastful manner.' (*al-Nisā* 4: 36)

In the final analysis, *iḥsān* boils down to *akhlāq* (character). A well-known supplication taught by the Prophet (peace be upon him) goes like this: 'O God, You have made my creation beautiful (*aḥsanta khalqī*), so make my character (*khuluqī)* beautiful too.'

It is *akhlāq* which, in turn, generates *'amal ṣāliḥ* (good deeds) as described in the aforementioned *āyāt*. The value of *iḥsān* cannot be overestimated since it is the *raison d'etre* of the creation of life. No more and no less: 'He Who has created death as well as life, so that He might put you to a test [and thus show] which of you is the most beautiful in conduct, and [make you realize that] He alone is almighty, truly forgiving.' (*al-Mulk* 67: 2)

At the end of the day, when people do what is beautiful, this of course is not for God's benefit. But rather people themselves gain by conforming to their own deepest nature. Doing *iḥsān* creates peace of mind and soul.

> *If you do what is beautiful, you do what is beautiful to your own souls, and if you do what is ugly, it is to them likewise.* (*al-Isrā* 17:7)

5

Conclusion (I): How to Achive Happiness

WHAT IS THE best way to actualize and nurture happiness in our lives? One's happiness will manifest when there is no discrepancy between what we long for and our actual state or circumstances. In this regard, people can carry out three kinds of effort in order to attain happiness.

First, work hard to pursue and accomplish whatever we desire in this life. At the very least, there are two faults in this approach. One, there is a high probability that we will never be able to fulfill *all* our wants and needs. Two, for every want or need that is met, a different one will always arise. Humans are insatiable. The Prophet (peace be upon him) said: '... for nothing can fill the belly of the son of Adam except dust (upon death and burial)'.[1] Therefore, with this approach we can almost be sure that it is impossible for us to ever feel that all our wants and needs are fulfilled. This approach will thus never bring happiness.

1. Narrated by al-Bukhari and Muslim.

Second, diminishing or suppressing our wants and needs. With diminished wants, the possibility of not fulfilling them becomes smaller and so too the possibility of our unhappiness. The problem is that God created humans with the aspiration to reach newer and better accomplishments. It is a manifestation of human *fitrah* (nature) to strive to attain perfection, however impossible it may be to achieve this perfection genuinely. Thus, before it can even attempt to bring happiness, this approach is already contrary to human nature. In other words, it is not realistic. And, all that is opposed to human nature will become a source of unhappiness.

Both of the approaches above are still based on the concept of extrinsic happiness. Namely, that happiness can only be achieved if everything we desire in life is achieved.

Third, having an inner attitude such that whatever happens or occurs to us, we are always grateful. Building an inner temperament bolstered by a patient attitude and unwavering gratitude will help curb the conditions that can potentially cause anxiety. This third point does not in any way nullify the first point above. Let us work hard, let us pursue perfection, to the best of our abilities. However, at any point in time we must be patient and grateful for what we have achieved, with full acceptance of whatever is allotted to us by Him. We will find happiness by always thinking positively in all circumstances, always seeking (positive) meaning behind every predicament, no matter how bad it appears to us.

However, this attitude should be supplemented by developing kindness towards others, especially to those in dire need of our help, through the spirit of giving. This is simply because to love, to give love, is the primordial nature of every human being. The tendency to be kind and giving resides in every human's heart since time immemorial.

6

Conclusion (II): Humans Were Born to Be Happy

According to Islamic teachings, it is the disposition as well as destiny of humans to be happy—and not to suffer as may be believed by some modern psychological schools of thought. If we wish to make a comparison, we can say that Islamic teachings agree more with 'positive psychology', which believes that humans are predisposed to be happy and what psychology does is merely unleash that potential. The foundation of Islamic teachings is the principle of the love of God, to such an extent that, like positive psychology, it rejects 'reparative psychology' theories such as Freudianism.

> *And by the soul and by Him Who perfectly proportioned it, and imbued it with moral failings as well as with consciousness of God! To a happy state shall indeed attain he who causes [this self] to grow in purity, and truly lost is he who buries it [in darkness].* (*al-Shams* 91: 7-10)

It is obvious that, according to the Wise Creator, a human being's natural disposition is to be happy. And, as has also been explicitly shown, happiness is closely related to the readiness or preparedness—or call it willingness—to be happy. To live happily, one must be completely ready to be happy, be willing to be happy. One must possess a mental attitude—or more accurately, emotional and moral attitude—to be happy. He or she must develop positive thoughts—towards life, and towards God, the Creator. That life has been designed by the Creator in the form of goodness, stemming from His love towards His creation. Viewed from a positive perspective, from a consciousness of wholeness, indeed life has no other characteristic but goodness. That, (what seems to be) suffering is nothing but goodness (as well)—albeit disguised. Difficulties are nothing but our failure to penetrate the outer layer, our inability to grasp the profound meaning of every occurrence. It is simply our failure to draw meaning from behind every phenomenon. And verily (what seems to be) hardship and misery are indeed a path to a higher goodness, that is happiness. Should we arrive at a roadblock en route to the goodness we have been pursuing, we should see it as merely a detour towards a path which, in fact, will lead us to achieving a greater goodness.

We could, quite often, obtain the meaning that we need by just slightly shifting our perspective on a given matter. Namely, equipped with the positive mindset that God has created us out of His great benevolence, and that we only need to endeavour to look at all problems with a positive viewpoint—any occurrence will bear within itself positive wisdom. Not only that, the essence of all happenings in the universe of God's creation is positive and brings benefits to us. To explain this, there is no clearer illustration than what was narrated by Dr. Victor Frankl, a psychologist widely known for his logotherapy method.

Once, according to Dr. Frankl, an old man came to his office. From his facial expression and body language, it appeared that he was burdened by an overwhelming sadness. He told Dr. Frankl that his very dear wife, who had been his life companion for decades, had just passed away. As a result, he felt that his life had no meaning anymore. All this time, he had shared his every happiness and difficulty with his wife. Without her, he lost the only person with whom he could share everything. If only he could, he would die to be with his wife.

Hearing this, Frankl told the poor man: 'Try imagining this, what would happen if your wife were always with you, until you died, leaving her behind? Yes, you would not experience the tremendous sadness that you feel right now, but what would have happened if you had died first, and your wife would have had to survive you?' The man was shocked and said, 'If that was the case, then my wife would be the one who would bear the overwhelming sadness.' 'Well,' said Frankl, 'the death of your wife that preceded yours, and the loneliness that you feel right now as the result, actually means that you have saved your wife from experiencing the tremendous grief that you feel now.' Hearing what Dr. Frankl said and pondering, suddenly a new awareness permeated the man. He realized that the sadness he felt now had a positive meaning of immeasurable magnitude, that is, to save his wife from tremendous grief. Thus, in stark contrast with the attitude he had when he came, he left Frankl's office in great bliss.

What distinguishes the situation of when the man came to Dr. Frankl's office with when he left? Indeed there was no change in the reality that he faced. However, he came in devoid of meaning in life, but left with a life full of meaning. And this amazing outcome ensued only because Dr. Frankl was able to help him shift his point of view *slightly* on the issue of his wife's death.

Indeed, God has provided human life on Earth with unlimited paths to goodness and happiness, that wherever we are facing and heading, there lies the road to our happiness.

Thus, this is the very character that we must develop and train, letting it evolve into a habit; in seeing and perceiving whatever happens in the course of our lives. Yes, it turns out that happiness requires training.

Train Yourself to Be Happy

First, heighten your realization and reinforce the knowledge that life is essentially good. Always reflect on your life and the lives of others. It is not at all difficult to see, with an open heart and mind, that there is always wisdom in whatever happens in our lives, and in fact in the lives of everyone, and this has always been the case throughout the history of humankind. Undoubtedly, evil is merely conceptual and essentially relative. An event, when seen in part rather than as a whole, may appear to be bad. However, once we observe the same event from a holistic perspective, it is in fact just a precursor to a greater good. Let us examine our experiences of life with a clear mind, and read the life experience of our neighbours, wherever and whenever we can with the intention of understanding the nature of this goodness. The more we believe in it, the more well-grounded our realization will become regarding the fundamental nature of goodness in the lives of God's creation.

Second, build our volition to see the bigger picture with positivity. This is not a difficult thing if we realize that our happiness is at stake here. Try always to look ahead, beyond the events themselves. Where will they lead us? What is their positive meaning? Then, establish a mental attitude (emotional attitude) of patience and gratitude. Always accept anything that befalls us with an open heart. Everything comes from God, and God, in His Infinite Wisdom, always looks out for our best interests. On what can be considered to be the other side of the same coin, always develop an attitude of gratitude, being thankful for whatever happens to us. Be grateful in any event, even if something is apparently a misfortune. You can do this by showing patience, and believing that the misfortune is actually a precursor to a higher goodness. By training yourself to react positively to adversity, you turn such experiences into an opportunity to develop a positive mind-set, which is the ultimate source of real happiness.

Third, train yourself to make a habit of happiness. Always seek full awareness and control over your emotional response to events that happen in your life. Over time, always let your happiness overcome your circumstances and never let events overwhelm you. Do not let panic rob you of your health. Any time an incident that feels unpleasant happens, try to search for meaning.

Dig deeper into the depths of your heart to find a positive meaning. Try to look for the silver lining, to determine which direction—to what goodness—the event will take you. Do it often and this attitude will end up being an instinctive response to any incident that befalls you.

Once we've tried the above mentioned strategies, then we can hope that happiness will always be with us without us having to chase it. In fact, happiness is always there with us. Anywhere, along with anything, there is happiness. Happiness is in our hearts. Our heart is created as a home for goodness, truth, and beauty which altogether beget happiness. Happiness will evade us if we go after it, because it does not belong outside us but within. We cannot pursue something that is not outside us, we just need to realize and understand what is inside us. We just need to say 'welcome' to happiness.

Concluding Note

As mentioned at the beginning of the discussion in this chapter, love is essentially a desire to give. On the one hand, it is said that love requires selflessness. However, if this means an absolute selflessness then where does the encouragement or even the longing come from? It is true that gifts which are based on true love must be sincere. Otherwise, what's the difference between selfishness and narcissism? Is not the essence of narcissism the urge to give for egoistic motives (ulterior motives) to gain benefits for oneself? How do we resolve this contradiction?

Actually, there is no contradiction here. Egoistic or narcissistic giving only happens when we expect something in return from the people who are the object of our giving. That is, we give something while hoping that there will be a reduction in the 'property' of the recipient, for the sake of ourselves. However, if happiness is what we expect—for those who realize it, happiness is really the highest reward for a sincere act of giving—then there is no demand on the part of the giver upon the object of our giving that may reduce anything on the part of the object. Happiness is derived from ourselves. As mentioned above, true happiness is intrinsic, not extrinsic. In this case, anyone is able to maintain a selflessness in their sincerity to give, but at the same time not losing the urge to give, because giving promises the highest rewards.'*Oh, Allah, I ask You for a life of happiness* (ḥayāt al-su'adā') *and a martyr's death* (mawt al-shuhadā').' *—Du'ā'* attributed to the Messenger (peace be upon him)

Part II

Life is an Odyssey of Love

I

Human Life: A Journey of Love

ONCE UPON A TIME, a reed was separated from its reed bed and it was born as a flute. It was troubled by endless grief and longing and whenever played, it lamented with heart-breaking melancholy. Separated from its source, it sang a song full of sorrow and yearning:

Listen to the lament of the reed-flute, forlorn
Ever since it was torn
From its rushy bed—a strain
Of impassioned love and pain.
'The secret of my song, though near,
No one can see and none can hear.'
Oh for a friend to know the sign
And enfold his entire soul with mine!
It is the flame of Love that ignited me,
It is the wine of Love that inspired me.
If only you knew how lovers bleed,
Listen, listen to the lament of the reed!

In this story, Jalāl al-Dīn Rūmī likens humans to a reed separated from its reed bed. We all came from God, but are separated from Him momentarily. 'Everyone separated from their origin, yearns for the time when they were united with it,' says Rūmī .

***

Indeed, human life, though few realize it, is actually an odyssey of longing. A journey starting with the descent, followed by a desire to return. Yes, our life is in effect a journey–from point of departure (*mabda'*) to a point of arrival (*ma'ād*)–which is infact the same as the departure point: humans originate and begin from God to return to God.

> *Innā li-Llāhi wa-innā ilayhi rāji'ūn. Indeed we belong to Allah, and indeed to Him we will return.* (*al-Baqarah* 2: 156)

We are created by–I could say emanated from–God and placed into the world in order to find our home back to Him.

In Islamic philosophy (*ḥikmah*), this is represented as one complete cycle of the journey of life, which passes two arcs that form a full circle: the downward arc (*qāws al-nuzūl*) from God to His creation (the world); and the upward arc (*qāws al-ṣu'ūd*) from His creation back to God.

As God reveals, the distance – or rather the absence of distance – between Him and His creations, represented here by the encounter of Muhammad (peace be upon him) on the occasion of *mi'raj* (the Ascension):

Thumma danā fatadalla. Fa-kāna qāba qawsayn aw adnā Then he drew near and drew close, until he (it) was two bows' length (*qawsayn*) *away, or nearer.* (*al-Najm* 53: 8–9)

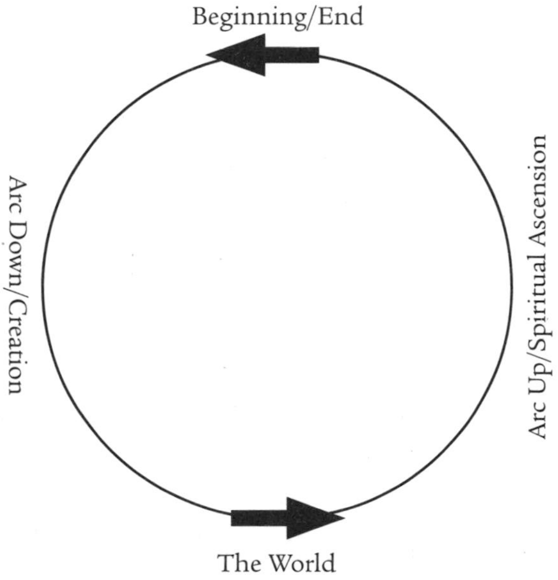

The two bows are the two halves of a complete circle. With a circle, one cannot designate the point of departure and the point of arrival. You can depart from any point and arrive at any point as well. Any point can be a point of departure or arrival. Both become one.

Thus, happiness lies entirely in how smooth the journey home is. By nature, man is at peace in the love of God, the Beneficent, the Especially Merciful. Separation is suffering and torment, although not many of us realize that.

We seek success and worldly pleasures *à corps perdu*—accumulating wealth, grabbing power, gaining popularity—which in reality conceals this longing. We think we will get the affection we so cherish when we possess all of those. In fact, they are just a mirage. Our happiness, our satisfaction, our tranquillity is not in them. What we seek is no less than reunion with God, one bound by love, God's ever-present love for us, and a love which we should develop for God.

Therefore, at stake here is how close we can get to Him, by trying to be like Him, trying to possess His attributes: our virtues taking the shape of His Virtues (*al-takhalluq bi-akhlāq Allāh*), the fashioning of our hearts to be full of compassion for others. Because only by nurturing our capacity to love others do we have a chance to obtain His love. His Messenger (peace be upon him) taught us: '*man lā yarḥam, lā yurḥam*'; which may be translated: 'Whoever does not love, will not be loved.'[1]

And His love lies in our compassion for fellow human beings, for fellow creatures of God. His Prophet (peace be upon him) said, in another hadith:

> *Whoever is kind to those on earth, will be shown kindness by those in the heavens.*[2]

However, during the long trip home to the Origin (*al-Mabda'*), we can still find a home on earth, among people who care for us. Our mothers, fathers, siblings, relatives, and friends: those who love us sincerely, on whose love we can rely. Their affections are actually the

1. Narrated by al-Bukhari and Muslim.
2. Narrated by Abu Dawud and al-Tirmidhī.

radiance of God's love; whose mercy illuminates the depths of their hearts. He is the source of happiness and peace in the world. We are guided home to Him at every opportunity. On the other hand, true to its actual meaning, estrangement from our beloved is a curse.

Life really is a journey back to God because it is from His Spirit that we are created (*al-Ḥijr* 15: 29). We are none other than His soul mates. And at the end of the journey, we are waiting for our true Beloved, God the Especially Merciful–only in His arms will all of our longings vanish; only in His care, will our yearnings be fulfilled.

> *O soul that has attained to inner peace. Return to your Lord, well-pleased [with your blissful destination] and pleasing [to your Lord]. Enter, then, together with My [righteous] servants, and enter My Paradise.* (*al-Fajr* 89: 27–30)

2

What is Love?

THERE IS A story about a pair of lovebirds, hailing from a noble background, consumed by the fire of love. Qays, the young man, was so captivated by his love that there was nothing in his thoughts but Laylā, his beloved. On the occasions he could not gaze at her, Qays would roam the streets and alleys looking for his beloved, calling out her name. Consequently, people started to laugh at him, addressing him with the epithet *Majnūn*, 'the madman'.

Circumstances brought their love to an impasse. Majnūn became increasingly oblivious to himself. This hitherto affluent youth started to live a destitute life—bedraggled, dishevelled and estranged from his community—he withdrew to live among stray animals. People would find him raving, uttering poems of love, beseeching the rivers and the breeze to convey his love to Laylā. Meanwhile, his beloved Laylā languished incarcerated in the confines of her room, tormented by an incessant longing for him. Even after being married off to another man, her soul remained with Majnūn.

To make a long story short, on the death of Laylā, when Majnūn found no other way to ease his pain, he gently laid his head on her grave and quietly gave up his soul. A year later, people found his lifeless remains on the tomb of his beloved, they had no option but to bury him next to his beloved as if to reunite them for eternity.

According to some narrations, it is said that soon after, a Sufi dreamt that Majnūn was by God's side. God was stroking him lovingly and said, 'Majnūn, were you not ashamed to call Me by the name of Laylā, after having consumed the wine of My love?' The Sufi woke up, distraught. If the Lord treated Majnūn so lovingly, he wondered, whatever happened to poor Laylā? Barely had the thought crossed his mind than God unveiled the answer to him: 'Laylā's position is exalted above all, for she kept the secrets of love concealed within.'

***

Love cannot be defined. At the very outset of his discussion about love, the great Sufi master, Ibn 'Arabī reminds readers of the fact that 'we must know that whatever can be known is divided into two categories. One category is for those things that can be defined, while the other is for what cannot. People who know and talk about love agree that it is included in things that cannot be defined. A person realizes love when it takes root within him, and becomes one with his nature. He cannot describe what it is but cannot deny its existence. The Shaykh categorized love amongst knowledge that can only be experienced. One cannot know it except through experience or feeling. Even after feeling, though, it cannot be explained to others. Hence, the Shaykh also said: 'People who define love have not understood it yet. And he who has not felt it by being immersed in it, has not known it.' Just as God can only be known by His attributes, similarly love cannot be known except in terms of the identification and description of its attributes and its name.

Love is too grand, said Rumi, to be defined. How does one define it when indeed the entire existence and life itself is love? There is nothing in this life that can define love. Rather it is love itself that defines life. In fact the term 'definition', here, is not appropriate at all; because, instead of delimiting and constraining, the love that encompasses this existence has no limits. How can it be limited when true love actually is (derived from) God Himself?

Love is a sensation that exceeds all limits. It is said that love is the true nature of God. And the love that exists in a slave is derived from that love. Know that the branches of love exist in eternity, with no beginning; and its roots also exist in eternity, with no end.

'People call you Love, I call you the Sultan of Love.'

'If I have to continue my explanation about love, I will have to cross a hundred cycles (of death) and resurrection before I would be able to complete it....'

Thus, due to this infinity of possibilities, Rumi admitted his helplessness to give words to love:

However much I describe and explain love, when
I come to love (itself) I am ashamed of that
(explanation).
Love cannot be carried or contained in words.
Love's an ocean of unfathomed depth.

Can the droplets of water of all the oceans be counted?
Yet the seven seas, next to the Ocean are infinitesimal.

In the end he could but only sigh:
How can I measure Your Ocean with my saucer?

According to al-Ghazālī, love can only be assessed by its fruits. So, what are the indicators of love?

The Prophet (peace be upon him) said:

> *The believers in their mutual kindness, compassion and love are just like one body. When one part of the body suffers, the whole body responds to it with loss of sleep and fever.*[1]

On another occasion, the Prophet (peace be upon him) is said to have taught that people who are in love remember their beloved a lot, and frequently call upon their name (*man ahabbashai'ankatsuradzikruhu*);[2] and as they say, a person is a slave to whatever he loves (*man aāabba shay'an fa-huwa 'abduh*).

The Prophet (peace be upon him), further said that the hallmarks of true love are threefold. The one in love:

1. Narrated by Muslim.
2. This is narrated by Abū Nuʿaym and al-Daylamī, but is considered a weak narration by the scholars of hadith, although the meaning is deemed sound.

1. prefers to speak with their loved ones over others,
2. tends to spend time with loved ones rather than with others, and
3. follows the wishes of their loved ones rather than those of others or themselves.

In the language of the Qur'an, love is called *al-ḥubb*. Al-Qushayrī, the author of the *Risālah*, describes *al-ḥubb* as the most pristine form of love and affection, as the Arabs say *ḥabab al-asnān*, referring to people with pure-white teeth. Al-Hujwīrī, the author of *Kashf al-Maḥjūb*, states that *ḥubb* is possibly from *ḥabb* which means seed. *Ḥubb* could therefore mean a love that lodges itself in the heart like a seed, unfaltering, and just like seeds scattered on the ground grow despite being assaulted by rain or scorched by the blazing sun, love continues to be a source of life. *Ḥubb* is also called so because it is derived from *ḥibbah,* which means a seed that bears fruit or a flowering seed. Love has been likened to a seed because it is the seed of life. Hence, a life without love is no better than death.

To illustrate the emptiness and untold suffering of a life devoid of love, Rumi laments: 'Know that a lover without love is like a fish out of water, dead and dry, even if they are the King.'

Lastly, the tremendousness of love is such that – as stated by the scholars – it obliterates arrogance and makes the ones afflicted by love humble themselves without hesitation. Love is a source of strength and concentration of attention; softening the heart, eliminating selfish interests in a person and making them generous and full of forgiveness.

On Love and Beauty
— Ibn ʿArabī (from *The Makkan Openings*)

PEOPLE HAVE A variety of opinions regarding love, even regarding its definition. Having found no one who can give its essential definition, we can conclude that it is beyond imagination. Every existing definition is merely referring to the results of love, its effects and its requirements; and is particularly related to the aspect of the Cherished Mighty One (al-ʿAzīz), who is Allah. Know that whatever can be known is divided into two categories. One category is for those things that can be defined, while the other is for what cannot be. A person realizes love when it takes root within him, and becomes one with his nature. He cannot describe what it is but cannot deny its existence. Know that love only exercises real control over those in love when it makes them deaf to anything apart from the words of the beloved, makes them blind to anything apart from the face of the beloved, and makes them mute except when mentioning the beloved.

What is love? Is it a description of a lover's very own self? Or is it an attribute within his spirit? Or is it a relationship between a lover and his beloved, in other words something that draws a lover tirelessly towards seeking union with the beloved? We consider it a description of the lover's own self. To those who object: 'But we can see it disappear', we respond that it can only disappear if the lover himself disappears from existence. How can a lover disappear because love does not disappear? All that can cease to exist is the relationship between a lover and a particular beloved, having been replaced by a relationship with another beloved. Hence, what exists is only a connection to any number of beloveds.... Love is the *rūḥ* (soul/spirit) of the lover and his core essence – not something that could disappear, or whose sovereignty could end. So the relationship between the lover and the beloved is just the connection whereas love is the lover's very essence.

We have divided the human characteristic of love into two kinds: carnal love which he shares with all the animals, and spiritual love which is altogether different. Carnal love is the love of ordinary people with its ultimate goal being the act of physical union. A union in which the passion of love permeates through the entire body just like water soaking into wool, or rather, like colour imbues anything being coloured. The key characteristic of this kind of love is that it's rooted in seeking pleasure and delight and hence, in reality, the lover loves the beloved only for his own sake, not for the sake of his beloved. There are many beloveds. Or rather, everything in existence is a beloved/ lover, but they do not know what their love is connected to. They are veiled by the being in whom they find their Beloved, imagining this being to be their beloved due to the domination of their carnal instincts.

He who loves women only in accordance with his carnal instincts doesn't really know the reality of his desire. For him she is mere form without a spirit, even though this form in its reality, is spirit. However, this truth is hidden from someone who approaches his wife solely for obtaining pleasure, without realizing whose pleasure it really is. If he knew the reality, then he could have known with whom he was obtaining pleasure, and only then would he have been perfect (in knowledge).

Spiritual love, on the other hand, is the soul's love, whose aim is to emulate the Beloved, acting according to the Beloved's rights over him and recognizing His decree. It is the love that unites the lover, in that he loves the beloved for the sake of the beloved and for himself. Know that spiritual love is when the lover is characterized by reason (*ʿaql*) and knowledge (*maʿrifah*). Through his reason he becomes wise and through his wisdom he becomes a knower. When he loves, he knows what love is, he knows the reality of the lover and the beloved; he knows what he desires of the beloved and what the beloved desires of him. Spiritual love must therefore equally deprive one of reason and make one no longer self-conscious. Its rapture is in the delight of spiritual knowledge, rather than carnal.

The one in love is suffering and tormented because he is a lover, and delighted because he is loved. The people of Paradise take delight in it because they are loved, whereas the prophets in this world unite both affliction and delight: their affliction comes from being lovers, while their delight comes from being loved.

There is also a third kind of love, which is divine love, i.e. the love of Allah for the servant and the love of the servant for Allah, as stated in the Qur'an (*al-baqarah* 2:117): 'He loves them and they love Him'. The greatest degree of this love is realized in two ways, first, when the servant sees that he is a locus for the manifestation of God's love, while it is God who is the Manifest. This is similar to how the spirit relates to the body, the spirit being always invisible and never to be seen. So he only sees Him as a lover. The second way is when God in some sense becomes the locus for the manifestation for the servant's qualities of love. This is realized when the servant becomes the beloved of God. However, as we have mentioned throughout, there is really no way in which love could really be known. We can only attempt to describe it in speaking or writing, but never truly know it.

Divine love consists in Him loving us for ourselves and for Himself. There is a Sufi tradition in which He expresses love for us for His sake: 'I loved to be known, so I created the world that I might be known to the creation, so that they, in turn, come to know Me.'[1] Thus

1. This statement occurs frequently in various Sufi texts and is believed by Sufis to be a hadith of the Prophet (peace be upon him). The great Sufi master Ibn 'Arabī states that this is an authentic hadith according to science of unveiling (*kashf*) although it has no foundation in terms of transmission (*naql*). Ibn Taymiyyah states that this narration is not known to be a tradition of the Prophet (peace be upon him) and that there are no chains of narration, neither weak (*da'īf*) nor authentic (Ṣaḥīḥ), illustrating his rejection of this tradition by scholars of hadith. Al-Zarkashī, Ibn Ḥajar, al-Sakhāwī, al-Suyūṭī, and others hold the same view (*al-Jāmi' fī al-aḥādīth al-qudsiyyah*, p. 375, no. 358). Mullā 'Alī al-Qārī holds the view that this tradition is sound in its meaning, and is in line with the Qur'anic statement '*wa-mākhalaqtu al-jinn wa al-ins illā li-ya'budūn*', which Ibn 'Abbas interprets as '*li-ya'rifūn*' (*Kashf al-Khafā*, vol. II, p. 1011).

He created us only for Himself, that we might know Him. His love of us for our sake is realized when we come to know Him through righteous deeds which lead us to our true happiness and deliver us from all that is not in line with our true purpose, or in harmony with our natural disposition. After all, has He not created creation to glorify Him?

Whoever limits love, does not know it! Whoever does not taste it by drinking, does not know it! Whoever says 'I was told about it' does not know it! Love is a limitless drink! One of the people of the unseen has said: 'I have drunk a drink, after which I have never been thirsty', to which Abū Yazīd responded: 'Here is a man who has drunk the oceans, and is still thirsty for more!' This is exactly what we have been alluding to.

Divine love is a spirit without a body; carnal love is a body without a spirit; spiritual love is body and spirit together.

3

Allah the Lover

A PIOUS MAN IS facing his Reckoning in the presence of Allah. Realizing that many of his family members have committed sins, the man decides to grant his reward for good deeds to the family members, up to the point that he runs out of his reward. God asks him: 'Now, how are you going to survive My *ḥisāb* (Reckoning)?' The man replies, 'I leave it to Your mercy, O Lord.' With that, God commands His angels to let the man enter Heaven.

***

At the beginning of every surah of the Qur'an, bar one, God refers to Himself as *Raḥmān* and *Raḥīm* – words that are generally translated as something like: the Most Gracious and the Most Merciful. However, the word *raḥmah* in Arabic, from which these two words are derived, has a very comprehensive connotation consisting of love, mercy, blessings and many other similar meanings. It is in this principle of love that the whole Islamic belief and way of life are summarized.

And it is not without a profound significance that a Muslim is taught to recite the same verse—'In the name of God, The Most Beneficent, The Most Merciful'—every time they embark on any endeavour, whether it has to do with religion or not. In the original Arabic, the expression uses the word 'Allah' instead of just any word denoting God. 'Allah' is actually His All-Encompassing Name (*al-ism al-jāmiʿ*) or His Greatest Name (*al-ism al-aʿẓam*) which both comprehends, and is the source of, all of His other names. In other words, notwithstanding the fact that His names comprise both attributes of beauty (*jamāl*) and majesty (*jalāl*), as one whole, the concept of God in Islam represents mercy and beneficence and nothing else.

(A side note: the words *Raḥmān* and *Raḥīm* are formed from the same root *r-ḥ-m*. Both signify compassion. But while *Raḥīm* signifies a specific form of compassion, i.e. (God's) compassion to the believers, *Raḥmān* signifies a general compassion, i.e. towards all creations, believers and unbelievers alike.)

In fact, love is the quintessential principle of God. He emphasizes in the Qur'an that:

> ... *surely my Lord is Ever Merciful, Most Loving.* (*Hūd* 11: 90)

In another place in the Qur'an, Allah is characterized by *wudd* (enduring love) and *ghufrān* (forgiveness) at the same time:

> ... *and He is the Forgiving and the Loving.* (*al-Burūj* 85: 14)

While His Attribute as *raḥīm* (merciful) and *wadūd* (loving) are mentioned together in this *āyah*:

> *Ask pardon of your Lord and then turn unto Him (repentant). Lo! My Lord is Merciful, Loving.* (*Hūd* 11: 90)

Further than that, in a *ḥadīth qudsī*, God reveals unequivocally that: 'My Mercy has overcome My Wrath.'

What is of the utmost importance is that all through the Qur'an Allah reveals Himself through these Most Beautiful Names (*al-asmā' al-ḥusnā*), those names denoting His Beautiful Qualities (*jamāl*) are found in five times as many verses as those that denote His Majestic Qualities (*jalāl*).[1] In the same vein, His Vengeance appears only once in the Holy Book, while the opposite quality–The Forgiving One–occurs about one hundred times.[2] Indeed, nothing in His creation is deprived of His Mercy:

> *My Mercy encompasses everything.* (*al-A'rāf* 7: 156)

1. There are traditionally believed to be 99 names of God (Allah), divided into the Majestic and the Beautiful. His qualities, such as The Vanquisher (*Al-Qahhar*), The Compeller (*Al-Jabbar*), The Supreme (*Al-Mutakabbir*) and The Avenging (*Dhu-'ntiqam*), are grouped into the former while the others, such as The Beneficent (*Al-Rahman*), The Merciful (*Al-Rahim*), The Lover (*Al-Wadud*), The Subtle (*Al-Latif*), The Forgiver (*Al-Ghaffar*) are grouped into the latter.
2. In the Qur'an (*al-Zumar* 39: 53), God even says that He: 'forgives sins, all of them.'

The last verse categorically states that all occurrences, not excluding things that appear to be evils and suffering, are actually manifestations of His Mercy.

Love as the Divine Creative Motif

God created the universe in the first place out of His love. According to a famous Sufi tradition: 'I was a Hidden Treasure (*kanz*). I loved to be known so that I created the creation in order that I become known (*u'raf*).'[3]

In a parallel tradition, He said: 'I loved to be known as the Forgiving, The Concealer of Disgrace, The Most Beautiful, The Most Beneficent and The Most Merciful; so I created the creation in order that I become known.'

The nature of the Essence, that is full of love and mercy, lies in revealing immense kindness, and in the outpouring of immense compassion. Every outpouring of love and compassion is destined for an object. It is in this overflowing of His love and compassion that the universe was brought into being—to be the object of this compassion.

This is how Sufis describe the reason for the creation of the universe. Love is the most basic principle of creation, *ab initio*. And it is this love that drives every creature on earth to strive to (re)unite with God by living a good life that would please Him.

Indeed, one of Allah's names, one of His attributes, is *al-Wājid*. This word has several meanings. Apart from having the meaning of intense, existential love, the word

3. This tradition, and the one that follows, have been discussed in footnote n. 1 above.

also means to bring into existence. Reflecting upon this divine name, we can see that there is a very close relationship between love and creation, in line with the aforementioned Sufi Tradition. Humans are here because of His love; the whole universe is here because of His love. This is what made the Prophet (peace be upon him) state in a hadith: 'God is Beautiful and loves beauty'[4]; and on another occasion: 'I saw my Lord in a most beautiful form!'[5]

From the Loving God, nothing originates except goodness. Even things that are apparently evil are in reality contributing to the creation of a greater good, thus manifesting His love to the universe. Again, His (apparent) Wrath–referring to the Sacred traditions quoted above–is in reality another facet of His Mercy.

4. Narrated by Muslim and Ahmad.
5. Narrated by al-Tirmidhī and Ahmad.

4

All Things are Signs of Love

ONCE THERE WAS a farmer who owned a magnificent horse. A very wealthy man ardently wanted to purchase it, even for an exorbitant fifty thousand dirhams. The farmer, however, politely declined the offer for he liked the horse for himself. His neighbours were flabbergasted that he had turned down such a lucrative offer. One day, unexpectedly the horse went missing. The people around him took to blaming him for the misfortune: 'You should have sold it for a high price when you had the chance; now you've lost it. What a great loss!' Hearing that, the farmer said, 'I know my horse is gone, but who am I to judge that it was a misfortune for me?' He chose to be patient.

A few days later the horse returned, bringing with it dozens of prize wild stallions for which the farmer was grateful. However, once again an ordeal befell him. For some reason, the untamed horses ran amok, accidentally trampling on his younger son, breaking one of his legs and leaving him incapacitated. Again, people took to blaming the farmer: 'Had you sold the horse, you would be rich, and your son would not be incapacitated.' Again, the farmer replied, 'Yes, my son is unable to walk, but I do not know if it was a misfortune.' Once again, the farmer preferred to be patient.

Shortly afterwards, a group of soldiers came to the village. The king had ordered them to conscript young people throughout the kingdom in order to send them into battle against the enemy. The farmer's son, being incapacitated, was left alone. Later, it was known that scores of young people who had gone into battle had become casualties of war. The farmer, once again, was grateful.

***

From God the Merciful, nothing radiates except goodness. Even things that seem bad are actually there to give rise to a greater good. They are a means to manifest His love in the entire universe. To reiterate, what looks like His wrath, is in reality, just another facet of His grace. In a hadith, the Messenger (peace be upon him) said, 'When God loves a group of people, He gives them trials.'[1]

Before anything else, God Himself declares that the universe and human beings are created in the best of forms, that everything from Him is good, and that everything evil is actually man-made or, more precisely, a distortion or corruption of divine virtues:

> *We have certainly created man in the best form.* (*al-Tīn* 95: 4)

1. Narrated by al-Tirmidhī.

[Hallowed be] He who has created seven heavens in full harmony with one another: no fault will you see in the creation of the Most Gracious. And turn your vision [upon it] once more: can you see any flaw? Yes, turn your vision [upon it] again and yet again: [and every time] your vision will fall back upon you, dazzled and truly defeated. (*al-Mulk* 67: 3–4)

God never oppresses humans in any way whatsoever; it is humans who oppress each other by acting to the detriment of themselves and the world.

Whatever good happens to you is from God; and whatever evil befalls you is from your own selves. (*al-Nisāʾ* 4: 79)

Verily, God does not do the least wrong unto people, but it is they who wrong themselves. (*Yūnus* 10: 44)

In another verse Allah clearly says:

... God would not change [goodness] which He had bestowed upon a people until they change what is within themselves. And indeed, Allah is All-Hearing and All-Knowing. (*al-Anfāl* 8: 53)[2]

---

2. This interpretation—which translates the word '*ma*' (the things) as goodness—is chosen by referring through comparison (*muqaranah*) with this next verse:

   Verily Allah would never change the blessings He has bestowed upon a community, except if they change what is within themselves. (*al-Anfal* 8: 53)

Indeed, trials are just God's way to determine the level (*maqām*) of a man's faith, to prepare him to enter Paradise, as among other things expressed in His words:

> *Or do you think that you shall enter the Garden [of bliss] without such [trials] as came to those who passed away before you? They encountered suffering and adversity, and were so shaken in spirit that even the Messenger and those of faith who were with him cried: 'When [will come] the succour of Allah.' They were assured: 'Behold, the help of Allah is [always] near!'* (*al-Baqarah* 2: 214)

In a *ḥadīth qudsī*, Allah even says:

> *When I love a servant, I test him [with difficulty and hardship] to make him call upon Me [so that the test is removed from him. And in this way, he gets closer to Me].*

So, once again, as expressed in the hadith quoted earlier, trials are truly nothing but a sign of His love.

Surely this, as revealed in several places in the Qur'an, is what is intended by God when He states that no matter how unpleasant the trials and difficulties seem on the surface, for the one facing the adversity there is in fact wisdom in them.

> *... perhaps you hate a thing and it is good for you; and perhaps you love a thing and it is bad for you. And Allah knows, while you know not.* (*al-Baqarah* 2: 216)

To be sure, as shown in the previous paragraph, Allah will provide help at the right moment. On top of that, He Himself has promised:

> *Allah does not charge a soul except [with that which is within] its capacity.* (*al-Baqarah* 2: 286)

Not only that, God promises rewards for those who are patient in accepting the ordeal:

> *We will surely test you with something of fear and hunger and a loss of wealth and lives and fruits, but give good tidings to the patient, who, when disaster strikes them, say: 'Indeed we belong to Allah, and indeed to Him we will return.'* (*al-Baqarah* 2: 155–156).

The good news is that the tests will bring us closer to Him in our journey back to Him.

A Note on Hell

Upon deeper analysis, Allah did not create Hell as a place of torture in which sinners get their punishment. In fact, all the difficulties that are inflicted in Hell are a trial (*balā'*), which serves to better the quality of a human being. And, considering all that comes from Allah is goodness, only those whose souls are polluted will fail to see the merit of this. To them, therefore, goodness will feel like torment.

In other words, human beings create punishment for themselves. Only the ones whose souls are ailing or tainted, because of their evil life in the world, will fail to appreciate the goodness of the trials as a means of purification of the soul. It is like someone who is already feeling hot, sitting in front of a blazing fire will feel intensely uncomfortable but for someone who is feeling cold the fire only provides warmth. In this regard, it should be understood that the word 'torture' or 'torment' is the translation of the word *'adhāb* in Arabic. This word is derived from the root word *'a-dh-b*. From the same root word comes *'adhb*, which actually means 'sweet', in other words: something good.

One way or another, the phenomenon of Hell remains within the framework of God's love. Doesn't God Himself say: 'My love encompasses everything?' Hell is not an exception to it. Punishment in Hell, as well as in the *barzakh* (isthmus)–even trials (*balā'*) in this world–is none other than *purgatorio* (Purgatory). It is where the human soul is cleansed, ensuring that the human is ready again to perceive Paradise as it is meant to be: namely, as a source of pleasure. Enter into it, back to Him.

Furthermore, according to some of the gnostics (*'urafā'*: those endowed with *ma'rifah*), the punishment in Hell is not eternal. First, some experts translate the word *abadan*, occurring in several verses of the Qur'an, not as 'eternal' but as 'centuries'. No matter how long it feels, it has limits. Even if we consider its meaning to be 'eternal', then–according to Ibn 'Arabī, among others–what is lasting is Hell, and not the punishment. The pronoun *hā* in the phrase *khālidīna fihā abadan* ('residing in it for all eternity') is referred back to the word *Hell* (*nār*, which is a feminine noun) and not to punishment (*'adhāb*, which takes the form of a masculine noun). In other words, *khālidīna fīhā abadan* should be translated as '(they) are in Hell eternally', and not 'they are in torment eternally'. There will come a time when Hell will lose its burning nature, just like the fire lost its burning and torturing nature in the case of Ibrāhīm (peace be upon him).

In fact, there are those who take the position that God would not be carrying out His promise to punish humans. Because, as God Himself states:

> *And the retribution for an evil act is an evil one like it, but whoever pardons and makes reconciliation, his reward is [due] from Allah.* (*al-Shūrā* 42: 40)

For those who hold this viewpoint, their question is, if God instructs us to have such a forgiving attitude, do you think He Himself will not forgive?

5

Allah's Love, Human Love

THERE IS A story of a pious woman who ended up as someone's domestic help. She had a habit of praying regularly every night. One day, the master overheard the prayers she uttered in her prostrations. She said: 'O Allah, I ask You with Your love for me to honour me with increasing devotion in my heart ...'. As soon as she had finished her prayers, the employer asked her: 'How do you know that God loves you? Why didn't you just say, "God, I call upon You with my love for You?"' She replied: 'O my master, were it not for His love for me, why else would He wake me up at hours like this? Were it not for His love for me, why else would He wake me to stand (*ṣalāt*) facing Him? Were it not for His love for me, why else would He move my lips to call upon Him?'

***

Islam indeed promotes a relationship full of love and yearning between man and God—just like the relationship of one who yearns and the one yearned for (*'āshiq* and *ma'shūq*).

As mentioned earlier, one of the words that the Qur'an uses to denote love is *wudd*, which, in Arabic refers to the highest form of love, and is mentioned in the Qur'an:

> *Indeed, for those who believe and do righteous works, the Most Compassionate Lord will create for them enduring love.* (*Maryam* 19: 96)

Al-Wadūd – *wudd* giving – is one of the Beautiful Names of Allah meaning a source of love. He has endowed human beings with an unlimited capacity to cultivate love.

In a number of verses, Allah states that love is supposed to underlie the relationship between man and God in a reciprocal manner—this time using another word that has similar meaning, i.e. *ḥubb*:

> ... *if any of you should ever turn away from your faith, remember that Allah will raise up a people whom He loves and who love Him* ... (*al-Mā'idah* 5: 54)

> ... *those who do believe are stronger in their love for Allah.* (*al-Baqarah* 2: 165)

The Prophet, through a prayer attributed to him by Imam 'Alī b. Abī Ṭālib—cousin and dear Companion of the Prophet, who is considered an early Sufi master—puts it very beautifully:

> *... Even if I endure the suffering (in Hell) together with Your enemies and You group me with those whom You choose to torment, and You separate me from Your beloveds and Your friends ... Even if I, O my God, my Master, my Companion, and my Lord, am patient in the face of torment, how could I ever endure parting with You ...*

This is perhaps the 'intimacy' of man and God which is conveyed in the following authentic *ḥadīth qudsī* which is very popular among the Sufis:

> *My servant performs the prescribed duties through which my servant comes close to Me. My servant continues to come closer to Me through the performance of supererogatory acts until I love him. And when I love him, I become his eyes with which he sees, his hearing with which he hears, his legs with which he walks, his mind with which he reflects and his tongue with which he speaks. When he asks Me (for something) I give him what he asks for.*

In fact, this 'relationship full of love' is what is meant by God when He says: 'And I did not create the jinn and mankind except to worship Me.' (*al-Dhāriyāt* 51: 56)

Ibn 'Abbās, one of the most learned Companions of the Prophet, is known to have interpreted the word *li-ya'budūn* (to worship God) as *li-ya'rifūn* (to know God). In other words, it is mandatory, and certainly the true purpose of creation, that we must always do our best to learn to know God.

Scholars and Sufis pushed on further with the exploration of the meaning of the word *'ibādah*, which is to worship. In Arabic, *ma'būdah*, which is the feminine of *ma'bud* (one who is worshipped), means woman who is idolized or beloved. It suggests that people who are madly in love are so badly in need of their beloved that they are ready to do anything to please whom they love. Just like a slave to his master or a worshipper to the worshipped. Naturally, people madly in love practically worship whom they love. In the final analysis, a survey of the use of the word *'abd* in the Qur'an, will find that it is always used to denote a person whom God loves, and who loves God.

Moreover, as revealed in the Sufi tradition on the Treasure (*kanz*), there is a connection between knowing and loving God. Did He not say that His desire to be recognized (*u'raf*) comes from His longing and loving?

It is but natural that all human beings long for a relationship with their God that is bound by such true love. It is from man to God, and vice versa. It is realized when all of our worldly selfhood has been annihilated by *mujāḥadah* (the struggle of the soul to cleanse itself of indulgence in worldliness); and when our soul has attained annihilation (*fanā'*) and has permanently lived (*baqā'*) in Him. Such a relationship is the ultimate goal of the complete human spiritual journey (to return to God).

6

Muhammad, the Prophet of Love

A STORY IS RELATED of a poor and humble old lady in a small town. She would seek any available menial task to make ends meet for herself and her family. Each afternoon she would go to the same mosque in order to clean the yard, picking up the leaves shed by the trees. That was her routine day after day, week after week, month after month and year after year. With time, she was no longer a stranger to all the congregants of the mosque.

One day, considering how old and frail the woman had now become, the congregants of the mosque took the initiative to clean the yard of leaves, which continued to fall. They did this in the hope of relieving her from a burden that was probably too much for her.

As usual, that day the old woman came to the mosque. How shocked she was to find the yard had been tidied up! To the congregation's amazement and regret, the old woman cried. When asked what in the world had made her so sad, she replied: 'I am already old, there is nothing I could do for my beloved Prophet. That is why I picked up the leaves to clean the yard of this mosque. However, that is not all that makes me sad. Each time I pick up a leaf, I send *ṣalawāt* to the Messenger of Allah. Now I have just lost one of the opportunities to express my love for him ...'.

***

According to Ibn ʿArabī, a man reaches his ultimate nobility–in accordance with the Sufi tradition: *takhallaqū bi-akhlāq Allāh*–when he adopts God's virtues. And Muhammad (peace be upon him), is the perfect manifestation of God's virtues. Once, when asked about the character of the Prophet, 'A'ishah (may Allah be pleased with her) said: 'The character of the Prophet was the Qur'an.' In fact, is not the Qur'an the perfect manifestation of God in the form of a decree?

Presumably, this is closely related to the fact that the most perfect *tajallī* (manifestation) of God's light is also within Muhammad (peace be upon him), as revealed in a Sufi tradition: 'The first thing created by Allah was Muhammadan Light.' In fact, in another Sufi tradition, it is stated that: 'If it had not been for you (Muhammad), I wouldn't have created this world.'

In other words, the perfection of the universe was manifested by God through the personality of the Prophet (peace be upon him) as the model. In the view of Ibn ʿArabī, the world is made possible through the manifestation of the 'ideas of God' which is referred to as *al-aʿyān al-thābitah* (permanent essences) that are a part of all of God's manifestations:

> *We will show them Our signs in the horizons and within themselves until it becomes clear to them that it is the Truth.* (*Sajdah* 41: 53)

And the Prophet Muhammad unifies all of them within him. Yes! Although virtually all humans are created as a model of the universe—that is, whereas the universe is the macrocosm (*al-'ālam al-kabīr*) and man is the microcosm (*al-'ālam al-ṣaghīr*), the Prophet is the most perfect microcosm representing all of His creation. That is also the reason why the Prophet is referred to as *al-insān al-kāmil* (the perfect human). God Himself, along with His angels sends *ṣalawāt* on him, then orders the believers to send *ṣalawāt* on him as well.

What is the essence of the perfection of the Prophet? God himself says of him:

> *... and indeed, you are of the most sublime character.* (*al-Qalam* 68:4)

And if we are to summarize all of the above, we can state that Muhammad's perfection lies in emulating the virtues of God (*al-takhalluq bi-akhlāq Allāh*).

Asked to describe the character of the Prophet, *Sayyidunā* 'Alī (may Allah ennoble his countenance) once said: 'Allah depicts the beauty of the world by mentioning: "Say, indeed, the beauty of this world is miniscule".' However, how does Allah describe the Prophet's morals? Allah says: 'And indeed you (Muhammad) have the most sublime character.'

So, what is the essence of the Prophet's morals? Love and affection, just like the character of Allah, Who in His

Holy Book states:

> *And it was by God's grace that you [O Prophet] deal gently with your followers: for if you had been harsh and hard of heart, they would indeed have broken away from you.* (*Āl 'Imrān* 3: 159)

However, above all other virtues of the Prophet, is his loving solidarity with humanity:

> *There has come unto you [O mankind] a Messenger from among yourselves: heavily weighs upon him [the thought] that you might suffer; full of concern for you [is he, and] full of compassion and mercy towards the believers.* (*al-Tawbah* 9: 128)

The Prophet's life was full of concern for all mankind. He always deemed human suffering as a burden. He wanted people to be free of the problems that afflicted them. On the other hand, he constantly hoped and strived so that every human being could live happily. It was such, that since his youth he had become the moral examplar of the society. Even before his marriage, he would go on spiritual retreats (*khalwah*) in order to find a solution to the ignorance of his people. No wonder that after becoming the Prophet and the Messenger of God, his entire life was devoted to the welfare of others. There was no estate for himself and his families on his deathbed, what he cried was only: 'My ummah (people), my ummah ... what will happen to them after me?' In the Hereafter, when human beings are gripped by the worries of the Reckoning, when even mothers will dump their babies, Muhammad (peace be upon him) would still only be thinking of his people.

On top of a hill he would call back and forth. '*Halumma halumma* ... come over here, come to me so you all have my intercession, be saved from His punishment, and you will all enter Paradise.' Indeed, Muhammad himself summarizes his character as love and mercy.

We must accept his loving nature and extraordinary leniency as an undeniable fact, given that God has said:

> *And We have sent you as nothing, [O Muhammad], except as a mercy to the world.* (*al-Anbiyā'* 21: 107)

He is the Messenger of the Entirely Merciful and Especially Merciful, the Sustainer and Preserver of the whole world. And above all, he is the perfect man *(al-insān al-kāmil)*, the perfect manifestation of Allah's merciful qualities.

He is the exemplar *par excellence* of God. He is a gateway for us to be able to return to Him. By following his path and making him our example, we are surely undergoing a process of spiritual ascension to develop *al-takhalluq bi-akhlāq Allāh* (qualifying ourselves with the virtues of God).

To love him is to love God and to love God is to love him. Just as the words of Allah taught him: 'If you indeed love Allah, follow me, and Allah will love you...'. (*Al 'Imran* 3: 31)

7

Ties of Human Love

THAT FRIDAY NIGHT he listened to the words of his mother, who stood in the corner of her room facing the *qiblah*. Ardently, he observed his mother praying dutifully–prostrating, bowing and completing the cycles of prayer. He was yet a child when he witnessed and heard his mother's prayer for all Muslims, men and women, calling their names, beseeching God to bestow fortune, happiness, and mercy on them. He waited painstakingly. Would his mother call upon God to ask something for herself?

That child was Imam Ḥasan (may the peace of Allah be upon him) who stayed up all night, not wanting to take his eyes off his mother, Fāṭimah (may the peace of Allah be upon her).

In eager anticipation, he waited to find out whether she would ask for something for herself while wondering what that might be.

As the lingering night turned into dawn, he was yet to hear his mother utter any words of prayer for her own sake, assiduously praying and supplicating for others.

In the morning he asked: 'Mother, last night I heard your words of prayer. I heard you praying for others, why nothing at all for yourself?'

His loving mother replied: 'My dear son, our neighbours take precedence over us.'

***

The bond of love that binds us humans to one another is expressed in Islam as *ṣilat al-raḥim*. It is a compound word derived from the words *ṣilah* and *raḥim* (womb). *Ṣilah* stems from a word that means 'to connect' or 'to attach' and is intended for those who are detached and scattered. Meanwhile, the word *raḥim*, originating from a meaning of 'mercy' (*raḥīm*), evolved to acquire the meaning of 'womb', since children in the womb are immersed in love and mercy.

In this regard, the Prophet (peace be upon him) relates in a *ḥadīth qudsī*: 'I am *al-Raḥmān*. I created the *Raḥim* (womb, i.e. family relations) and derived its name from My Name. Hence, whoever maintains it, I will keep ties with him, and whoever severs it, I will sever ties with him.'

It has been narrated that on one occasion a Bedouin Arab came to the Prophet (peace be upon him) during one of his journeys, and said: 'Tell me the things that will bring me closer to Paradise and keep me away from Hell.' The Messenger of God replied: 'Worship Allah and do not ascribe any partners to Him, offer prayers perfectly, pay the zakat and maintain good family relations.'[1]

1. Reported by al-Bukhari and Muslim.

So important is the *ṣilat al-raḥim* that in His Holy Book, He said:

> *... who break their bond with God after it has been established [in their nature], and cut asunder what God has commanded to be joined, and spread corruption on earth: these it is that shall be the losers. (al-Baqarah 2: 27)*

Ṣilat al-raḥim is often understood as keeping or maintaining good relationships, even if it is only by visiting one another or communicating with each other in a variety of ways. The true meaning of *ṣilat al-raḥim* is more expansive. *Ṣilat al-raḥim* means all the efforts made in doing good–righteous deeds–to others and all the deeds we do to make people happy, especially to help relieve people from the burdens weighing them down. It is not restricted to relatives and people close to us, although Islam emphasizes that we put family and those close to us first, but extends to all mankind, even to all the inhabitants of the universe.

The Prophet (peace be upon him) stated: 'Be loving (merciful) to those on the earth, so the One above the heavens will be loving (merciful) to you.'

In the same vein, according to a weak hadith he also stated: 'All creatures are the dependents of Allah, and Allah loves most those who treat His dependents well and kindly.'[2]

'What is the best of Islam?' the Prophet (peace be upon him) was asked, to which he replied: 'To feed (the

2. Narrated by Abu Ya'la.

hungry) and greet those whom you know and those whom you do not.'[3]

So important is *ṣilat al-raḥim* that on one occasion the Prophet (peace be upon him) taught us: 'God assists His servant, so long as his servent is assisting his brother (i.e. fellow humans).'[4]

When all is said and done, manifesting *ṣilat al-raḥim* like this, in the form of good deeds that help ease human difficulties, would ultimately reinforce the bond of affection between human beings.

> *Indeed, for those who believe and do righteous works, the Most Compassionate Lord will create for them enduring love.* (*Maryam* 19: 96)

It is narrated that Allah asked Mūsā: 'O Mūsā, which deeds of yours are for Me?' Mūsā replied: 'Truly all my deeds are for you, O God!' 'No, O Mūsā!' Allah replied, 'Indeed your deeds are for you yourself.' Mūsā asked: 'Then which of my deeds are for you, O God?' God replied: 'Imbuing happiness into the hearts of the heartbroken.'[5]

Companions of the Prophet Muhammad (peace be upon him) heard him say: 'Allah (*subḥānahu wa-ta'ālā*) said: "Those who love one another for My glory, will have platforms of light, and the Prophets and martyrs will wish that they had the same".'[6] Indeed, the Prophet also advised us: 'You will not enter Paradise ... unless you love each other.'

---

3. Narrated by al-Bukhari and Muslim.
4. Narrated by Muslim.
5. Narrated by Abu Nu'aym al-Isfahani.
6. Reported in al-Tirmidhī.

In advice to his companion who was named the governor of Egypt, Mālik al-Ashtar, Imam 'Alī stated: 'Develop in your heart the feeling of love for your people and let it be the source of kindliness and blessings for them. Do not stand over them like a greedy beast who feels it is enough to devour for yourself that which belongs to them. Remember that the citizens of the state are of two categories. They are either your brethren in religion or your brethren in humanity.'

Actually, love and affection are akin to benevolence, as opposed to avarice. Love is a principle that puts our needs and interests beneath the needs and interests of our loved ones. In fact, it is due to love that we are willing to put aside our own needs and interests for the sake of those we love. This is the underlying philosophy of love and affection. Allah says in the Qur'an:

> *... They love those who have migrated to them and do not covet what has been given them; they even prefer them above themselves though poverty be their own lot. And whosoever are preserved from their own greed, such are the ones that will find true happiness* (mufliḥūn). (*al-Ḥashr* 59: 9)

Through acts of giving and doing good to our fellow humans, we will merit His love. According to a weak hadith the Prophet (peace be upon him) said: 'All God's creatures are His dependents; and he or she is the most beloved of God who tries to be most beneficial to God's creatures.'[7]

7. Narrated by Abu Ya'la and al-Tabarani.

Lastly, on another occasion, the Prophet (peace be upon him) said: 'I saw a bond of relationship (*raḥim*) attached to the throne (*'arsh*) of Allah, complaining about one who cuts it off.' [8]

These teachings show how important it is that we treat all people right, no matter how far removed we might be in terms of kinship.

8. Narrated by Abu Ya'la and al-Tabarani.

8

Marriage as a test of *Iḥsān*

IT WAS NARRATED that Abū Ṭalhah harboured a love so deep for Umm Sulaym that he decided to ask for her hand. Umm Sulaym's answer, however courteous and deferential, was crushing: 'Speaking frankly, it does not behoove me to turn down a suitor like you, O Abū Ṭalhah. Alas, you are a nonbeliever and I'm a Muslim woman. We are not eligible to get married. Try to surmise what I really want?'

'You want wealth and comfort,' said Abū Ṭalhah.

'Not in the least!' exclaimed Umm Sulaym emphatically, 'All I want is that you embrace Islam right away.'

'But who will guide me?' asked Abū Ṭalhah.

'Without a doubt that will be the Messenger of Allah (peace be upon him) himself,' said Umm Sulaym.

So Abū Ṭalhah rushed to meet the Prophet (peace be upon him), who at the time was seated with his Companions. Upon seeing Abū Ṭalhah approach, the Prophet exclaimed: 'Abū Ṭalhah is drawing near you all and the light of Islam gleams in his eyes.'

Umm Sulaym's sincerity touched the depths of Abū Ṭalhah's heart. She only wanted to marry him for his Islam without the slightest hankering for the comforts that he promised. Could any woman other than Umm Sulaym deserve to be his wife and the mother of his children? In the presence of the Prophet, Abū Ṭalhah repeatedly uttered: 'I follow your teachings, Messenger of Allah. I bear witness that there is no God worthy of worship but Allah and I bear witness that Muhammad is the Messenger of Allah.'

So, Umm Sulaym married Abū Ṭalhah, with a *mahr* consisting only of her husband's Islam. This prompted Thābit–the narrator of this hadith to declare: 'I have never heard of a woman whose *mahr* is more praiseworthy than Umm Sulaym's, which is her husband's faith in Islam.'

***

> *And among His wonders is this: He creates for you mates out of your own kind so that you might incline towards them, and He engenders love and tenderness between you: in this, behold, there are messages indeed for people who think!* (*al-Rūm* 30: 21)

In the verse quoted above, Allah presents marriage as one of His signs. So we ask, what signs? Surely all things good, true and beautiful are signs of God–for He Himself is the Good, the True, the Beautiful. Nonetheless, amongst His signs, there is none greater than love. For indeed, what encompasses and sustains all the attributes of God is love. God is love, as is indicated in Islamic scripture. Before moving any further with this discussion, however, let us look at another dictum of God in regards to the aforementioned question:

> *And of everything We created pairs; perhaps you will remember [the greatness of God].* (*al-Dhāriyāt* 51: 49)

The word 'pairs' is the translation of the word *zawjayn*, whose root is the same as that of *zawāj* (meaning marriage). The original meaning of this word is 'to unite into one, to complete'. In other words, before the pairing occurs, the component halves have yet to achieve fulfilment or completion; they are still fragmented. In the case of man, the state of being 'incomplete' or 'fragmented' engenders a longing for the missing element, which would make his erstwhile self no longer unfulfilled or fragmented.

And hence, the longing of a man for a woman, and vice versa, is a sign (as well as a reminder) for the longing that should be present in the Man-God relationship: God's love for mankind and the universe, and man's love for Him. True love with its essence of the joy of being devoted to a loved one, which should also be developed in marriage, will give a glimpse of the love and longing that characterize the relationship between all creatures and their Origin.

> *Those who have attained faith love God more than all else.* (*al-Baqarah* 2: 165)

Indeed, Allah has created man imbued with the nature to love Him. Do humans not retain within them a breath of His spirit, a part of Himself? So, like droplets of water, whether it be water from rivers, rain water or morning dew, humans always long to return to the sea, to the Origin. Undoubtedly, man's true soul mate is Allah. It is only the physical aspects of his nature, and his attachment to the carnality of a self continually beguiled by lust, that cause him to forget his true Beloved.

To reiterate: marriage, worship and true love, which are supposed to blossom into a congenial marriage, are a manifestation of a hallowed and loving relationship between man and Allah. They are beacons which in turn, at the very least, should remind every man and woman, who love each other, of their true love.

Hence, marriage in Islam has a very deep spiritual import, not just because it is an act of channelling human sexuality restrained within the etiquette of Shariah, nor because it takes the form of a loving relationship solely encouraged in Islam, rather it is much deeper than that. Marriage is a sign of God through which a person is reminded of the Divine and all-consummate relationship with his true Beloved.

This is why the Prophet (peace be upon him) said: 'Three things from your worldly life have been made dear to me, namely: women and fragrance, but the coolness of my eyes is in prayer.' He mentioned prayer at the end because prayer is the ultimate goal of all three. That is, women (wives) and fragrances comfort and strengthen his heart.[1] Thus, it is with a strengthened heart that he busied himself with worship (prayer) and attained the coolness of his eyes (joy).

Aside from being a means for humans to procreate while living their lives in accordance with religion, marriage is also a means of obtaining peace and tranquillity. But, above all, it is an avenue to reach the highest of our life's goals, which is to pray and to worship Him, in accordance with His words:

1. According to al-Ghazali, a human heart obtains serenity and intimacy by conversing with its partner. This tranquillity can help increase devotion to worship because observance of prayers can drain energy and cause fatigue. Tranquillity obtained in this way helps restore the heart's worship. *Sayyiduna* 'Ali said: 'Let not your heart be burdened by overexertion and fatigue, such that it becomes blind.'

   Sometimes, the Messenger of Allah felt a heavy burden in his soul when he received revelation. He would hold A'ishah's hands and say: 'Talk to me, A'ishah.' Then, he regained his strength and his energy for resuming his preaching and worshipping God would recharge and he would say: 'Delight us, O Bilal,' then he would return to prayer.

And I did not create the jinn and mankind except to worship Me.[2] *(al-Dhāriyāt 51: 56)*

---

2. There is an important difference between a Sufi thinker like Imam al-Ghazali and a gnostic (*'arif*) like Ibn Arabi. Although recognizing the benefits of marriage as a means of gratification, Imam al-Ghazali tends to view conjugal relations as legitimate only to the extent of channelling the desire that was created by God in order to procreate. In contrast, Ibn Arabi holds the view that sexual intercourse in a marital relationship, albeit transpiring with candid sexual intent, at its zenith, nonetheless, brings a healthier awareness of the Divine, and aims to bring immense happiness. In this context, Ibn Arabi states that the power of sexual intimacy (*qahr al-ladhdhah*) that dominates, subjugates and subdues its subjects will teach both spouses a sense of *'ubudiyyah* (servitude or submission) to God. This is the *'ubudiyyah* which at its peak is in line with the meaning of the verse about the creation of man quoted above. This is also the secret of why God describes happiness in Paradise, among others, in the form of sexual pleasure. If we follow the view of Ibn Arabi, it becomes clear that, instead of seeing conjugal relations (of husband and wife) as simply a necessity, Islam sees it as something sacred. Indeed, Islam only sees sexual intercourse as something bad if it is not done in the frame of the Shariah. Besides, how could we say that sexual intercourse is bad when it is based on love, which is no less than spiritual in nature?

Various Types of Love[1] —Ibn Ḥazm

Ibn Ḥazm al-Andalusi (994–1064), has interestingly elaborated on the various forms of love:

> *I have been asked to focus on what there is to say about love, and the different kinds of love. All the different kinds of love belong to the same root. Love is characterized by a sense of longing for the beloved, a fear of separation, and a hope of reciprocation. It is suggested that the sentiment varies in accordance with the object. But the object varies only according to the degree of the desire of the lover, whether it is strengthening, weakening, or even fading away. Thus, love felt for God Almighty is perfect love, a love that unites His creatures in a quest for the same ideals.*

1 Extracted, with modifications, from Abu, Laylah M., *In Pursuit of Virtue: The Moral Theology and Psychology of Ibn Hazm al-Andalusi [384–456 AH/994–1064 AD];* with a Translation of His Book *Al-Akhlaq wa'l-Siyar* (London: Ta-Ha Publishers Ltd., 1990).

Love—of parents, children, husbands, wives, friends, rulers, benefactors, lovers, anyone who becomes a haven of hope—is one and the same, everything is love. However, there are differences in each that I have mentioned. They differ in the magnitude of a love that is inspired by what can be offered by a loved one. Therefore, love can take many forms: We have seen people die broken-hearted because of their children, just like a lover who might have his heart broken by his beloved. We have heard of people who were so overcome by fear as well as love of God that they died of it. We know that people may become jealous of their kings and friends, the same as husbands who become jealous because of their wives; lovers because of their beloveds.

The least level of desire experienced by someone towards his/her lover is the desire to win their love and attention, and to get closer to them—without expecting anything beyond this. This is the aspiration of people who love each other for the sake of Allah.

The next level is when love grows in togetherness, conversation and mutual interest. This is the degree of love that we have for kings, friends or brethren.

However, the height of what a lover may wish from his beloved is to embrace her in his arms whenever he desires her. This is why a man who passionately desires his wife would attempt various positions and locations during their love-making, wanting to possess her more completely. In this category we include caresses and kisses. It is this aspect of love that resides in a father toward his children, encouraging him to (express) it through hugs and kisses.

The abovementioned is uniquely the function of (extreme) desire. If, for some reason, a desire for something is being suppressed, the soul will turn to another object of desire.

Consequently, we find that people who believe in the possibility of seeing Allah will always long for it, have great yearning for it, and will not be satisfied by anything less, since that is what they truly desire. On the other hand, those who do not believe in it will not aspire to this ecstasy since they do not wish for it, not having any desire for it. It will be enough for them just to perform *ṣalāt* (ritual prayer) and go to the mosque. They do not have any other ambitions.

Part III

Sources of Happiness

I

Sanctity of *Fiṭrah*

IT IS SAID that while on his deathbed, a very evil tyrant, during whose reign the subjects lived in abject misery, summoned the prime minister of the kingdom and decreed: 'After my demise, cremate my mortal remains and strew the ashes over the seven seas.'

Despite his heinous misdeeds, it seemed that the tyrant's human disposition had spoken to him. He was beset by the fear of being brought to Reckoning (*ḥisāb*) in the presence of Allah. Reportedly, due to his fear Allah forgave his sins and granted him Paradise.

***

> *... turn your face single-mindedly to the true Faith and adhere to the true nature on which Allah has created human beings. The mould fashioned by Allah cannot be altered. That is the True, Straight Faith ...* (*al-Rūm* 30: 30)

The word *fiṭrah* in Arabic is derived from the root word *f-ṭ-r*, meaning 'to originate something that did not exist.' In other words, *fiṭrah* is 'something that was originated and without precedent.' Its synonyms are *al-khalq* and *al-ibdā'*. For example, the first drops of milk coming out of a camel are called *fiṭr*. So in the above verse, *fiṭrah* means the human aspect that was first created. Not only that, this aspect will never change throughout one's life—in other words, it is everlasting. It is also no accident that another meaning of the word *fiṭrah* is 'being imprinted or welded', with the meaning that once imprinted or welded, the change is permanent and cannot be undone.

Above all, it is important to acknowledge that, in fact, the innate human aspects are moulded on the archetypal nature or the 'Essence'—that is *fiṭrah*—God's own.

Furthermore, as stated in the verse above, *fiṭrah* is identical to religion itself—'the correct religion'. This is the sound worldview (*weltanschauung*) and natural way of life, whose orientation is directed towards faith in God and in the truth—a point of view and way of life—which in the beginning of the self-same verse is called the way of life that is *ḥanīf*.

Upon further analysis we discern that *fiṭrah* has two predominant and fundamental components. First, faith in God as our Lord, as our Creator and our Caregiver:

> *[Remember] when your Lord drew forth from the Children of Adam from their loins—their descendants—and made them testify concerning themselves, [saying]: 'Am I not your Lord (who cherishes and sustains you)?' They said: 'Yea! We*

do testify!' [This], lest you should say on the Day of Judgment: 'Of this we were not aware.' (*al-A'rāf* 7: 172)

The second component of *fiṭrah* is the knowledge of good versus evil that has been revealed to humans since the beginning of their creation:

And by the soul and [He] that formed it [in accordance with what it is meant to be]. And gave it with discernment of its wickedness and its righteousness. He will succeed who purifies it, and he will fail who instils it [with corruption]. (*al-Shams* 91: 7–10)

We can conclude, based on the aforementioned analysis, that every human being is created with an innate tendency to believe in Allah, and an innate knowledge of piety and goodness as well as evil. Yet, more importantly, the fullness and meaningfulness of our lives–our happiness–lies in our success in maintaining the sanctity of our faith in Him and our ability to perform good deeds and avoid the bad ones–the knowledge of which has already been revealed to us. Our failure to do so–in this case, our turning away from God and the lack of orientation towards good deeds in our lives–will deplete our heart, leaving us desolate, no matter how abundantly we surround ourselves with possessions and people. After all, is it not that these predisposed tendencies in our lives have become *fiṭrah* (innate nature) and are thus inalterable?

That is why the Prophet Muhammad (peace be upon him) said: 'Righteousness is that about which the soul feels at ease and the heart feels tranquil. And wrongdoing is that which causes unease and unhappiness in the soul.'[1]

Live by relying on your *fiṭrah* so that you will be happy.

1. Narrated by Ahmad and al-Darimi.

2

Coming Closer to Allah

A MAN WHO DID not believe in the existence of God once came to Imam Ja'far al-Ṣādiq and challenged him: 'What evidence do you have that God exists?' Imam Ja'far ordered his companions to throw the man into a lake. The poor man was not much of a swimmer. As he started to drown, he screamed for help: 'O Ja'far, help me!' However, the Imam forbade his companions to help that man. As the drowning man flailed about, losing hope and fearing for his life, he wailed in desperation: 'Oh God, help me.' Imam Ja'far promptly ordered his rescue from the lake and then said to him: 'God is He whose name you call upon, when you are sure none can help you but Him.'

***

Why is it, that in order to be happy, humans need to be close to Allah? First, the question of religion has been a human concern ever since the first humans walked the earth. The American philosopher, William James, was a leading proponent of Pragmatism. He wrote his book, *The Varieties of Religious Experience*, more than a century ago, in 1902. Although not a religious man himself, he concluded that despite culture and civilization dragging humankind in disparate directions, people who pray and draw near to God will be, rather paradoxically, larger in number. No matter how many people a man surrounds himself with, he/she will never live happily until he befriends *The Great Socius* (the Supreme Comrade), God! This was also the thesis of a myriad of other researchers in religion, including the Nobel Prize winning biologist, Alexis Carrel, in his two classic works: *Prayer* and *Man, The Unknown.*

Contemporary sociologist, Peter Berger, was obliged, in his book *The Desecularization of the World*, to revise his outlook from his previous works, regarding the disappearance of religion from human life. In fact, a number of predictions claiming that religion would die out have all failed. In 1945, *Time* magazine published a cover story in which it predicted that the demise of religion was only a matter of time. Sixty years later, in another cover story, they admitted that their prediction was wrong. Religion, in fact, has experienced a strong resurgence. Even *Newsweek* demonstrated that despite pursuing materialism and secularism, increasing numbers of Americans prayed more as compared to exercising, watching movies and even having sex.

Undoubtedly, it is clear that God dwells in the *fiṭrah* (the primordial nature) of these creatures known as human beings–no matter how much atheists are constantly trying to deny it.

Certain atheists offer an explanation of God as the 'God of the Gaps'. That is, God whose presence is solely to fill our inability to explain our circumstances. If we are in a quandary to explain why the universe is filled with cataclysms that we are unable to prevent, we devise a concept of God that could explain it. So, fear and ignorance have driven people to create (the concept of) God.

There is also a concept which Richard Dawkins calls the *meme*, a kind of gene, but social rather than biological. As people inherit genes from their parents, this 'social gene' is also passed around society by the social environment. God, in this context, is a kind of inherited legacy of a social environment.

The truth is, be it called *meme*, gene or 'God of the gaps', humans are definitely in need of something–that is then referred to as God, Allah, Yahweh, Sang Hyang Widi and so on. In fact, since primal times more than 180 centuries ago–even with manifold advances in science and technology–what is known as God has never ever disappeared from human life.

Germane to this, the Prophet said: 'Allah created Adam on His Form/Image'[1] Man was created on the basis of the 'nature' of divinity. So, God is the source and model of man. Similarly, He taught us that: 'Indeed we belong to Allah, and indeed to Him we will return.' (*al-Baqarah 2:156*) There is a bond that unites man and God. God is in fact the human's soul mate. 'But those who believe are stronger in love for Allah.' (*al-Baqarah* 2:165) so states the Qur'an.

Regrettably, the physical form which envelops our spirit often masks our *fiṭrah* with lustful and egotistical

1. Narrated by al-Bukhari and Muslim

tendencies, making us forget our true nature–the knowledge that our real soul mate is Allah. As a consequence, in this world, if we are far from Allah, it is not necessary that we will always feel melancholy. It is especially true for those who have blinded their insights. However, the day we will move to the *barzakh*–where our spiritual prowess is enhanced–we would grieve in anguish because of having lived a life that kept us away from Allah. And upon resurrection–when the spiritual veils will have been lifted–all the more so. At that moment would we come to the realization that our True Love is Allah. Regarding this moment, Allah says, 'but now We have lifted from you your veil, and sharp is your sight today!' (*Qāf* 50: 22), and '*Wa-ḥuṣṣila mā fi al-ṣudūr*' 'and that within the breasts is revealed' (*al-'Adiyāt* 100: 10). Thus, the most important thing to be revealed is that our love is Allah. As a result, when we are faced with the reality that Allah is away from us; that is certainly Hell. Whereas Heaven is our proximity to Him, cultivated by blessings attained by being victorious over our lust and ego. Indeed, according to some Sufi translations, Hell is a condition in which a man is plagued by profound sorrow because he is far from Allah, whereas Heaven is the union with Allah.

The paramount happiness is achieved when our love is requited, when our soul is replete with love. And the most sorrowful plight is the emptiness of unrequited love–primarily, our love of God. In other words, Paradise is going back to Allah while Hell is being away from Allah.

3

Becoming Accustomed to *Dhikr Allāh* (Remembrance of Allah)

IT IS RELATED that Rābiʿa al-ʿAdawīya was hurrying along the streets of Baghdad one afternoon with a pail of water in one hand and a burning torch in the other. Someone asked, 'Rābiʿa, where are you going?' She replied, 'I'm going to light Paradise on fire and pour water to put out the fires of Hell so that people stop worshipping God out of fear of Hell or desire for Paradise!' And also, alone under the silent skies at night, she would pray: 'O my Lord, every lover is alone with their beloved, and here I am alone with You, yearning for Your love.'

***

> *[People who turn to Allah are] those who believe, and whose hearts find their rest in the remembrance of God—for, verily, in the remembrance of God hearts do find their rest—[and so it is that] they who attain to faith and do righteous deeds are destined for happiness [in this world] and the most beauteous of all goals [in the life to come]! (al-Raʿd 13: 28–29)*

The above verse teaches us that those who believe in the existence of God with all His Mercy, and those who always remember Him and are habituated to doing good deeds—that is, all efforts to make our environment better—are the ones who are happy, both in this world and in the Hereafter.

In another place, Allah says:

> *(Those conscious of Allah are those) who believe in [the existence of] that which is beyond the reach of human perception, and are constant in prayer, and spend on others out of what We provide for them as sustenance; And who believe in that which has been bestowed from on high upon you, [O Prophet,] as well as in that which was bestowed before your time: for it is they who in their innermost are certain of the life to come! It is they who follow the guidance [which comes] from their Sustainer; and it is they who shall attain to a happy state!* (*al-Baqarah* 2: 3–5)

The conformity between the two verses above shows that always being conscious of Allah (having *taqwā*) and doing *dhikr* are very much related. That is, an inner attitude of belief in and constant consciousness of God will, as a consequence, inspire the holder of this attitude to always perform good deeds for Allah's pleasure, which at its peak effects constant remembrance of Allah. In turn, the remembrance of Allah, an Ineffable Essence Most Compassionate and Merciful, on Whom we can depend with total faith that He will always apportion goodness to us, is the inexhaustible source of our true happiness.

It is probably easily understandable. The unshakable faith in the existence of people or beings with a genuine love for us so sincere that we can completely depend upon them, and who are willing to do anything for our welfare–be it our mother's love, the love of our spouse, not to mention God the Almighty's love–will comfort us and make our lives fulfilled. Antithetical to that is misery, a desolate and isolated state comprising not only of loneliness, but also of dread stemming from a life bereft of meaning and purpose. This is what is termed, in religious parlance, a state of being accursed or damned, causing human suffering. This, in all likelihood, is also the meaning of the Paradise and Hell to come–a tranquil fulfilled life versus a stifling desolate one.

We should not be oblivious to the fact that faith, *taqwā*, and remembrance of Allah in its true sense can never be attained unless accompanied by good deeds, acts of giving and helping others. In fact, the real test of our faith in Allah lies in our readiness to give to, and help others. Without it, our faith or religiosity will be a blatant lie:

> *Have you seen the one who denies the religion? For that is the one who drives away the orphan. And does not encourage the feeding of the poor.* (*al-Mā'ūn* 107: 1–3)

Instead of achieving peace and contentment, those who are reluctant to give would be flung to a life of adversity and repression:

Thus, as for him who gives [to others] and is conscious of God, and believes in the truth of the ultimate good, for him shall We make easy the path towards [ultimate] ease. But as for him who is niggardly, and thinks that he is self-sufficient, and calls the ultimate good a lie; for him shall We make easy the path towards hardship. (*al-Layl* 92: 5–10)

4

Manifesting Allah's Attributes

JADHĪMA AL-ABRASH, an Arab king, never undertook any endeavour without first conferring with the Roman Emperor who was one of his closest friends. Once, intending to seek the Emperor's opinion regarding his children's future, he sent a letter to him in which he wrote: 'I feel I should set aside a fortune for each of my sons and daughters in order that they do not fall into tough times after me. What do you think?'

The Roman Emperor replied: 'Your fortune is an allurement–unfaithful and impermanent! The best service for your children would be to enrich them with noble character and laudable traits, which will guide them to permanent leadership in the world and forgiveness (of sins) in the Hereafter.'

***

According to the hadith quoted before, Allah created human beings on His Form/Image (*'alā ṣūratihi*). The hadith, as interpreted by the exegetes, informs us that human beings are endowed by Allah with a wealth of Divine attributes, which, handled scrupulously, will have room to grow and manifest themselves. They comprise of Absolute Goodness, Absolute Truth and Absolute Beauty. In the subsequent paragraphs we will attempt to elucidate how to develop these traits inside us.

First, love righteousness and goodness. In Islam, anything that is good is called *al-ma'rūf*, while vile and evil things are termed *al-munkar*. *Ma'rūf* means matters that are well-known and in accordance with preexisting knowledge within human nature. While *munkar* consists of whatever is shunned by the human heart. The Prophet (peace be upon him) discernibly delineated the difference between *ma'rūf* and *munkar* in one of his sayings. He stated that goodness is something that our heart recognizes and accepts; whereas evil is something that the human heart innately rejects. That is why truth is called *ma'rūf* (what is already well-known), while evil is called *munkar* (what is repudiated).

As such, humans are intrinsically aware of and able to distinguish between good and evil. Regrettably, for one reason or another, we are often complacent about filling our hearts with sufficient goodness. Whereas one of the prerequisites of happiness is drawing near to Allah, which denotes that we are steadfast in goodness.

Second, love of truth (*al-ḥaqq*). The subsequent requirement, in order to be happy, is to be faithful to the truth, as Allah is *al-Ḥaqq*. *Al-ḥaqq* means truth that is not even faintly tarnished with falsity of any kind. So, if we wish to draw near to Allah, we should always strive to be objective people. Objectivity will present itself only when we are able to overcome our ego. However smart and full of wits, if a person is ruled by his ego, he cannot be wise or intelligent. On the contrary he will make a fool of himself.

Third, always appreciate beauty. Allah is Beautiful and He loves beauty. It is mentioned in a hadith, '*Inna Allāh jamīl yuḥibb al-jamāl*', or to put it more philosophically, Allah is Beauty Itself. Therefore, every human being needs to nurture a continual relationship with beauty, and the beauty that is close to Allah is the inherent beauty of nature. Allah says: 'We will show them Our signs in the horizons and within themselves.' (*fussilat* 41:53) In the Qur'an, Allah frequently depicts nature among the signs of His Greatness.

Germane to this, the Prophet (peace be upon him) once said, 'I saw God in the Most Beautiful Form.'[1]

According to Ibn 'Arabī, nature is actually man's 'brother'. Nature is sometimes called *al-insān al-kabīr* (human on a grander scale), while man is called *al-'ālam al-saghīr* (the microcosm). That is, in another sense, man is a small universe in terms of size while nature is 'a grand depiction of man'. Allah has created the universe and human beings with precisely the same principles.

Since humans are actually very close to nature, they will yearn for it each time they are separated from its beauty. For instance, look how city-dwellers love beautiful natural scenery and they yearn for it. Likewise, villagers living for so long in the city miss the natural beauty of their village, as has been proven by modern research.[2]

1. Narrated by al-Tirmidhī and Ahmad.
2. Ricard, Matthieu. *Happiness: A Guide to Developing Life's Most Important Skill*. London: Atlantic Books, 2015.

This indicates that human nature is characterized, among other things, by its love of beauty.

For Allah has created the universe as a 'brother' of human beauty and we should appreciate the aesthetic aspect of nature. The closer we are to beautiful things the closer we are to Allah.

However, even higher than the beauty of nature is the beauty of the imagined world and the spiritual world. The beauty of the imagined world manifests itself in the beauty of sublime works of art. At the same time, despite being at a loss for words to describe spiritual beauty man can experience it, producing fulfilment and immeasurable happiness.

Thus, human beings were created with an innate nature to love goodness, to love the truth and to love beauty. If these three things do not bring fulfilment to his *fiṭrah*—his heart, his spirit—it is completely impossible for him to attain true happiness.

True happiness will materialize when we seek to do good, to love the truth and to always love beauty. The more we strive to pursue these three conditions, the closer we are to Allah, resulting in a greater predisposition towards happiness. And Allah knows best.

Reaching the Ultimate Happiness with Allah[1] —Al-Ghazālī

LOVE OF GOD is the most important topic, and is also the ultimate goal, of our discussion so far. We have been talking of spiritual dangers because they hinder love for God in the human heart. We have also talked about the good characteristics necessary for it. The perfection of humanity lies here; love of God must conquer and rule man's heart completely.

Even if love of God is not in full control, then it should be the greatest feeling in one's heart, overcoming love for others. Nonetheless, it is easy to understand that love for God is something that is hard to attain, that a school of thought in the science of *kalām* (theology) denies that man can love a being that is not of his own species. They defined love for God as a simple act of obedience. Indeed, whoever thinks so does not understand what religion truly is.

1. Al-Ghazali, *Meramu Kebahagiaan* (Jakarta: Penerbit Hikmah, 2002), pp. 107–124.

All Muslims agree that to love God is an obligation. With regard to the believers, Allah says He loves them and they love Him. And the Prophet (peace be upon him) said: 'Unless you love Allah's Prophet more than you do others, you do not have true faith.'[2] Some commentators note that when the angel of death came to take his life, Ibrāhīm said: 'Have you ever seen a friend taking the life of his friend?' God answered: 'Have you ever seen a friend displeased with meeting with his friend?' So Ibrāhīm said: 'O,'Izra'īl, now take my life!'

The Prophet (peace be upon him) taught his companions the following prayer: 'O, Allah grant me Your love, the love of those who love You, and the love of that thing which brings near Your love. Make Your love dearer to me than cold drink is for the thirsty'.[3]

Ḥasan Baṣrī often said: 'Those who recognize God will love Him; and those who recognize the world will adopt renunciation.'

Now we will discuss the essential nature of love. Love can be defined as the inclination towards things that give us pleasure. This is evident with respect to our five senses, each of which love everything that gives them pleasure. So the eyes love beautiful shapes, the ears love music, and so on. This is the kind of love that is also possessed by animals. However there is a sixth sense, namely the faculty of complex perception, which is rooted in the heart and not possessed by animals. Through this sense we become aware of beauty and spiritual excellence. So, someone who is only familiar with the pleasures of

2. Narrated by al-Bukhari and Muslim.
3. Narrated by al-Tirmidhī and Ahmad.

the five senses cannot understand what was meant by the Prophet (peace be upon him) when he said that he loves praying more than he loved fragrances and women, although they were also dear to him. Conversely, a person who opens his eyes to see the beauty and perfection of God would deem all those visions as trifles, no matter how beautiful they seem.

Humans who are only familiar with the pleasures of the senses would say that beauty is in a rainbow of things, in a harmony of body parts and so forth, while they are blind to the moral beauty intended by people when they talk about whoever has a good character. People who have a deeper perception are more likely to be able to love the great people who have lived before our time—like the Caliph 'Umar and Abū Bakr—for their noble qualities, although their bodies have long ago been engulfed in dust.

Such love is not directed to the outer shape but to the spiritual qualities. Even when we want to evoke a child's sense of love for others, we do not describe their outer beauty—we describe their spiritual excellence instead.

If we apply this principle to our love for God, we will find that He is the One that is most lovable. If someone does not love him, it is because he does not recognize Him. We love something in a person because that something is a reflection of Him. For this reason, we love Muhammad (peace be upon him). He is the Prophet and the love of God; and love for the knowledgeable and the pious is really love for God. We shall see this more clearly when we discuss the causes of love.

The first cause is the love of man for himself and the perfection of his own nature. This leads directly to love for God since all of man's fundamental entity and nature are nothing but the grace of God. If not for His goodness, man would never have emerged from behind the curtain of non-existence into this visual world. Preservation and attainment of human perfection are also entirely dependent on the mercy of God. It is strange for someone to look for protection from the hot sun under the shade of a tree when the tree itself doesn't exist at all. Similarly, were it not for God, man would not have come into existence, let alone have his own character. Therefore, he who does not know that he comes from God cannot love God. The fool cannot love Him because love radiates directly from the knowledge of Him. When does a fool have this knowledge?

The second cause of love is the love for something that benefits him, and in fact the only one who benefits him is God; because the benefits that a man does to another are really benefits brought about by God through him. Any motive that drives a person to do good to others, be it a motive to obtain merit or a good reputation, is also compelled by God.

The third cause is love that is awakened through the contemplation of the nature of God, of His power and wisdom. When compared to this love, all of the power and wisdom of man, is nothing more than a reflection in its most trivial qualities. This love is similar to the love we feel towards those great men in the past, such as Imam Mālik and Imam Shāfiʿī, although we never expect to receive personal gain from them. Therefore, this e kind of love is more selfless. God revealed to the Prophet Dāwud; 'The dearest of My dear persons is that servant who worships Me without receiving any favour from Me and who fulfils his duty to God most faithfully.' In the Gospel it says: 'Who is a greater sinner than one who worships Me in greed of Paradise and in fear of Hell? If I had not created Paradise and Hell, would I not be entitled to be worshipped?'

The fourth cause of love is 'similarity' between man and God. This is what is meant in the words of the *ḥadīth qudsī*: 'My servant continues to draw near to Me till I love him. When I love him I become his ears with which he hears, I become his eyes with which he sees, and I become his tongue with which he speaks.'

God also said to Mūsā: 'When I was ill why did you not come visit Me?' Mūsā replied: 'O Allah, You are the Lord of the heavens and the earth; how can it be that You were ill?' God said: 'One of My servants was ill; and you did not come to see Me. To see him means to see Me.'

Indeed, this is an issue that is rather dangerous to discuss because it is beyond the understanding of ordinary people. Even someone who is intelligent can stumble when deliberating this issue and believe in incarnation or partnership with God. Although there are those among theologians that argue humans cannot love a being that is not of their own species; in fact, no matter how great the distance that separates them, man can love God because of the 'similarity' that is suggested in the above words.

To See Allah

All Muslims claim to believe that seeing God is the pinnacle of human happiness as it is stated in scripture. For many people, however, this claim is simply a theory that does not evoke a feeling in the heart. This is natural because how can we long for something we do not know? We will try to explain that seeing God is the greatest happiness to be attained by humans.

First of all, all humans have their own potential, with its own pleasure and its own goodness, from the lowest of bodily lust to the highest form of intellectual understanding. However, even the lowest form of mental effort will result in greater pleasure than that of the highest physical lust. So, it is no wonder that someone who is absorbed in a game of chess, will not bother to eat although repeatedly reminded. The higher our knowledge is, the greater the pleasure we get from it. For example, we get greater pleasure in obtaining secret information about an emperor than a vizier. And since knowledge of God is the highest object of knowledge, the pleasure gained from the knowledge of God is also greater than the pleasure gained from the knowledge of others. People who know God, while in fact still living in this world, will feel they are already in a Paradise 'as wide as the heavens and earth'–a Paradise whose fruits are so delicious that nobody can stop picking them; a Paradise that will never be cramped no matter how many the number of inhabitants.

However, the pleasure of knowledge is still lower than that of sight, just as our pleasure in imagining our beloved is much lower than the pleasure gained through meeting them in person. Yet, our imprisonment in our own flesh and bone and our engagement in sensory pleasure have created a curtain which prevents us from seeing God, although they do not prevent us from gaining some knowledge of Him. For this reason, Allah said to Mūsā on Mount Sinai: 'You will not be able to see Me.' (*al-A'raf* 7:143)

The truth of the matter is as follows. As the seed of man will grow into a man and a date palm seed will grow into a palm tree, the knowledge of God gained in this world will be transformed into a vision of God in the Hereafter, and those who never learn the knowledge of God will never experience the vision. This vision will not be divided equally between those who know, but the level of clarity will vary according to their knowledge. God is One but He will be seen in many different ways, just as an object is reflected in various ways by different mirrors—some are diffuse, some clear, and others obscure. A mirror may be damaged, and one may bring a heart that is so dark and dirty to the Hereafter, that the vision which becomes a source of happiness and peace for others, for him will merely be a source of sorrow. Someone whose love for God in his heart prevails over his love for others will inhale more happiness from this vision than one whose love is not so intense; such is the case with two sharp-eyed people staring at a beautiful face. The one who has loved the owner of the face will be happier to look at it than one who has not. To be able to enjoy a perfect happiness, knowledge alone, without love, is not enough. Love of God cannot fill a human heart before the latter is cleansed of love for the world which can only be obtained through *zuhd* (renunciation).

In this world, the human condition with respect to the vision of God is like a lover who is about to see his beloved in the dim light of dawn, while his clothes are swamped with bees and scorpions which constantly torture him. However, once the sun has risen with all its beauty, and the venomous animals have stopped torturing, the joy in seeing the Creator will be like the happiness in seeing the beloved and being freed from disaster in this world and seeing Him without a veil. Abū Sulaymān said: 'He who today is busy with himself will also be busy with himself tomorrow; and he who is preoccupied with his Lord today, will be preoccupied with his Lord tomorrow.'

Ambition and arrogance are diseases that blind our hearts. They block our love for God and hinder us from seeing the vision of God. It is narrated that Allah said to 'Īsā: 'O 'Īsā, if I see in the hearts of My servants pure love for Me that is not stained with the selfish passions for this world or the world to come, then I will be the guard of that love.' And when people asked 'Īsā to reveal the most noble deeds, he replied: 'Love God and surrender yourselves to His will.'

The saint Rābi'a was once asked about her love for the Prophet of God. She said: 'My love for the Creator has prevented me from loving His creation.' Ibrāhīm ibn Adham said in his prayer: 'O God, with the honour given to me by Your love, Your satisfaction toward me by Your remembrance, the value of Paradise is like the wing of a fly.'

People who think that it is possible to enjoy happiness in the Hereafter without love of God have gone too far astray, because the core of future life is to come to God as the long-desired object and the destination, which can take us an immeasurable distance to arrive. Happiness is the joy of having love for God. He who does not have love for God today will not rejoice in seeing God tomorrow. And if happiness in our love of God today is small, we will feel the same degree of happiness tomorrow. In short, our happiness in the Hereafter will be exactly the same as the levels of our devotion to God today.

Na'ūdhu bi-Llāh (we seek refuge in Allah), for someone who has cultivated in his heart love for something that is in conflict with his love for God, will find the state of the Hereafter to be completely strange. What makes other people happy will make him sad.

It can be explained through the following anecdote. A carrion-eating man went into a market that sold perfumes, and upon sniffing the pleasant fragrances there he instantly fainted. Hoping to make him come around, the onlookers began to crowd around him, splashing rose water on him and bringing *misk* (perfume) up to his nose, but to no avail. In fact it made him even worse. Finally someone, who was also a carrion-eating scavenger, came along. He pushed the first man's nose into trash and the man recovered immediately, sighing with satisfaction. 'Wow', he said, 'this is what I call perfume!' So, in the Hereafter, man will no longer have the obscene pleasures of this world; spiritual happiness in the Afterlife will be completely new to him, and will even lead him astray. Because the Hereafter is a spiritual world, and is a manifestation of the beauty of God, happiness there is only for people who have been chasing Him and are drawn to Him. All renunciation, worship and questions will turn into a goal, and that goal is love. This is the meaning of the verse in the Qur'an: 'He who nourishes [his soul] will surely be successful.' (*al-Shams* 91:9) Sins and lust are directly disadvantageous to the achievement of this.

Therefore, the Qur'an says: 'And he who corrupts [his soul] will surely come to grief.' (*al-Shams* 91:10) The people who were bestowed with spiritual insights have understood this truth as a real experience, not just a traditional proverb. Their crystal-clear experience on this truth brings them to the belief that people who carried the Truth were really prophets, the same as someone who has studied medicine will easily be convinced by a doctor. This is a kind of belief that does not need support in the form of extraordinary miracles like those practised by sorcerers.

Signs of our Love for God

Many people claim to have loved God, but each must examine the purity of that love themselves. The first test is that they should not hate the thought of death because a 'friend' is never afraid to see another friend. The Prophet (peace be upon him) said: 'He who wants to meet God, God wants to meet him.'[4]

It is true that a sincere lover of God may be afraid of death before completing his preparations for the Afterlife. But if he is sincere, he will be diligently preparing for it.

The second test of sincerity is that one must be willing to sacrifice his will for the sake of God's will; must hold on tight to what brought him closer to God; and must keep away from places that push him to be away from God. The fact that someone has sinned is not proof that he does not love God at all; it only proves that he does not love Him with all his heart. Al-Fuḍayl b. 'Iyāḍ said to someone: 'If you are asked, "Do you love God?" keep silent, because if you say, "I don't love God," you will

4. Narrated by al-Bukhari and Muslim.

become an infidel. If you say, "I love God," the attributes of those who love God are not found in you.'

The third test is that *dhikr Allāh* should constantly be fresh in one's heart. Because, if someone is in love, he will always remember his beloved; and if his love is perfect then he will never forget Him. Of course there are times when one's love for God does not occupy a major place in the heart, but love for God in fact remains, because love is one thing, and love of love something else.

The fourth test is that a man will love the Qur'an as the word of Allah, and Muhammad as the Prophet of God. If his love is really strong, he will love all human beings because they are all the servants of God. His love will include all of creation because people who love someone love anything and everything about them.

The fifth sign is that he will have a thirst for *'uzlah* (solitude) for the purpose of night prayers. He will constantly crave the arrival of nights to get in touch with his friend without hindrance. He who takes more pleasure in useless conversations and sleep than he takes in solitude cannot claim that his love is perfect.

It is narrated that Allah said to Dāwud: 'Don't love anybody among My creation as I shall deprive two persons from My favours: he who slacks in rendering night prayers if there is a delay in receiving rewards for good works, and he who forgets My favours and immerses himself in his base desires. The sign of this is that I leave him to himself.'

Actually, if love for God truly overwhelms human hearts, then all other love will be lost. One of the Children of Israel built a place to pray at night. However, once he knew that a bird used to sing beautifully at the top of a tree, he prayed under the tree in order to enjoy the pleasure of listening to the bird, God told Dāwud to go and tell him: 'You have attached yourself to created things, I will lower your rank.' On the other hand, some people love God in such a way that when they are engrossed in worship, they would not know if their houses were on fire.

The sixth sign is that worship becomes easy for him. A *walī* said: 'The first thirty years of my night prayers were a great difficulty, but thirty years later it has been a pleasure for me.' When love for God has reached its perfection, no happiness can surpass the happiness gained in worship.

The seventh sign is that lovers of God will love him and hate those who reject God and those who do not obey, as the Qur'an says: 'They are severe toward the those who reject God, and sympathetic among themselves.' (*al-fath* 48:29)

The Prophet asked God; 'O God, who are your lovers?' His answer came: 'Those who cling tightly to Me just as a child to his mother, who take recourse to the remembrance of Me as an eagle takes refuge to its nest. They express anger at sins, just as a fearless tiger does when enraged.'[5]

5. Narrated by Ahmad in Kitab al-Zuhd.

5

Developing Contentment (*Riḍā*) (I)

ONCE, A KING, accompanied by his aide, went hunting. As luck would have it, the king met with an unfortunate accident and lost one of his fingers. This saddened and upset him. The aide, in all innocence, entreated the king to be grateful despite what had befallen him, reassuring him that there was a silver lining behind everything that occurs. Upon hearing this, the king was enraged and ordered his aide be imprisoned.

After a while the king went hunting again, this time by himself. On his way to the forest he was ambushed by a horde of ferocious natives with primitive beliefs, who captured the king, intending to sacrifice him to their gods. Fortunately for him though, missing a finger made him flawed and rendered him unfit for sacrifice; an offering to their gods had to be perfect. So they decided against sacrificing him and let him go instead.

On his return from the misadventure, the shaken king pondered over the truth of his aide's statement and immediately granted him his freedom. Upon meeting his aide, the king was grateful but said: 'There still is a slight niggle of doubt in my heart regarding what you had said. True, there is wisdom in the accident which cost me one of my fingers, but what is the wisdom behind your imprisonment?'

The aide replied: 'Had you not imprisoned me, my lord, without a doubt it was I who would have been sacrificed to their gods.'

The attitude of recognizing whatever befalls us as goodness, full of wisdom, and accepting it is commonly referred to as *riḍā* (contentment).

***

In various Sufi writings, *riḍā* is often referred to as the highest *maqām* (station) in the spiritual journey. This is because contentment is a direct manifestation of faith. A dialogue between the Prophet (peace be upon him) and his Companions confirms this.

One day the Prophet (peace be upon him) asked his Companions: 'What is the hallmark of your faith?' They replied: 'We are grateful in times of good fortune, patient in the face of adversity and remain content with *qaḍā* (what was decreed).' The Prophet said: 'By the Lord of the Ka'bah, then you are truly believers.'[1]

How can it not be? Through gratitude and patience, *riḍā* no longer differentiates what comes our way be it a calamity or good fortune.

Allah says: '... And indeed your Lord is going to give you so amply that you will be completely content.' (*al-Ḍuhā* 93: 5) For those who possess the characteristic

1. Weak hadith narration al-tabrani.

of *riḍā*, whatever comes to them (from God) is a blessing. All that comes from God is always good, the difference is believed to be only in the packaging. What appears to be a calamity is also a blessing in disguise; it just appears to be a misfortune because of the way it is packaged. In other words, it is just a matter of perception.

Whoever has, within themselves, instilled contentment, believes that behind all apparent disasters indeed lies wisdom. Such calamities serve merely as a harbinger to the arrival of blessings. They sometimes serve as a redirection steering us precisely towards what we have been seeking.

In a verse of the Qur'an, God teaches us to believe that:

> ... *Nothing befalls us save that what Allah has decreed for us* ... (*al-Tawbah* 9: 51)

While in another verse, Allah says:

> *Whatever good befalls you [O man] it is from Allah, and whatever ill befalls you it is from your own self.* (*al-Nisa'* 4: 79)

Juxtaposing these two verses, and with the fundamental belief that the verses of the Qur'an do not disagree with one another, we are lead to the conclusion that everything that comes our way is inherently good. Namely, everything comes from God, and everything that comes from God is good. It is our own perception that makes (part of) it look bad (that is to say, appear to be a calamity).

Thus, someone who has reached the mental state of contentment will always be able to look beyond the packaging and into the essence of the things that happen to us, and will believe—even live—it as a gift of goodness.

In this regard, this following *ḥadīth qudsī* becomes very relevant: 'I am as My servant thinks of Me.'

If we believe everything that comes from God is good, then it will in fact turn out to be good for us. Thinking well of Allah is another aspect of the state of *riḍā*.

Ultimately, those who have reached the level of contentment described above will be willing to accept whatever comes to them. Thus, their heart will always beat peacefully and they will be satisfied with whatever happens to them. This is none other than happiness.

As spoken by the Prophet: 'Verily, Allah, with His justice and His knowledge, puts welfare and joy in contentment and faith, and puts suffering and sorrow in doubt and disappointment.'[2]

Or in the words of the Sufi, 'Abd al-Wāḥid b. Zayd: 'Contentment is the most expansive of God's portals, Heaven in this world and an abode of true worshippers.'

2. Narrated by Abu Nu'aym al-Isfahani.

6

Developing Contentment (*Riḍā*) (II)

ARTHUR RUBINSTEIN, a prominent twentieth century Polish composer and pianist, always looked cheerful and optimistic, emanating an aura of happiness every day. His friends were curious as to his secret.

On his eightieth birthday, responding to his friends' request, Rubinstein revealed the secret: Every morning, as he opened his eyes, he imagined himself like a new born baby. As a result, he always felt that his life was full of things to be learnt, to be explored. Consequently for Rubinstein, life became an arena that was both vitalizing as well as challenging.

As his life progressed beyond the age of eighty, his vision started to fade, as happens when one gets old. With his eyesight progressively deteriorating, it was getting harder and harder for him to play the piano and his eyes were no longer able to control the movement of his hands hitting the keys. People surmised that Rubinstein's career as a pianist would soon be over and his expertise would wane. Likewise, they thought his signature happiness, which always accompanied him would vanish, sooner or later.

After all, wasn't playing the piano his life? In the eyes of many people, it was time for Rubinstein to lose his joy and happiness. But, lo and behold, what happened instead?

Rubinstein remained Rubinstein, still retaining a colossally happy demeanour. Precisely at a time when his vision was increasingly getting blurred, and even after becoming totally blind, he felt that his life was even more vitalized. He felt that he had received a new challenge from God, a new grace, having achieved everything that he ever wished for in life. What was it? Learning to play the piano without looking! In contrast to what people had in their mind, Rubinstein was even happier, even more passionate than ever. Rubinstein was among the few who were able to make their lives radiate happiness, under even the most difficult circumstances. His perspective on life is, sadly, not shared by many people.

***

Indeed, since Allah created the universe out of His love this whole cosmos has been designed as His best creation. In other words, the original propensity of this world is to grant the greatest benefit and happiness to its inhabitants. As a consequence, He revealed a variety of possible courses–including the ways out of difficulties–to the point of perhaps being infinite. This universe is a set of roads and opportunities toward the highest good, perfection and human happiness.

If one day we are experiencing a certain set of circumstances, treading on one of the roads, we need to remember that it is merely one amongst many of

His infinite pathways. If, on the current path, we can achieve the goodness we have been pursuing, God be praised, otherwise many other roads are available to lead us towards the goodness and happiness we have been longing for. So, if we are not successful with one road, we just need to change track. Therefore, not only can we attain the happiness that we seek through the infinite choices of alternative roads, our 'failure' will actually make us more experienced, more intelligent and more mature. Most likely, we will eventually find a level of happiness which is higher than the happiness we would have achieved if we had succeeded in our original attempt. This is also why this condition is sometimes called a 'blessing in disguise'. Or sometimes we are taught, 'every cloud has a silver lining'. But as a matter of fact goodness is not in disguise, the reality being that there are actually no dark clouds. There is only a bright clear sky that at that moment is blanketed by condensation. Goodness and blessings—I should write 'goodnesses' to indicate a plurality that has no limit—are real, we just do not recognize them until after we are stuck on the road on which we are currently travelling.

This is also the meaning of the verse:

> *And, behold, with every hardship comes ease: verily, with every hardship comes ease!* (*al-Sharḥ* 94: 5–6)

The exegetes, based on the fact that Allah repeats the same verse twice using the definite article '*al-*' (the) for 'hardship'('*usr*) in both verses and not using it for the word 'ease' (*yusr*), state that the verses should be understood as: 'Along with (the same) hardship, comes a lot more ease.'

This is precisely the positive meaning of the trials, tests and calamities. They are a part of His compassion, or His way of opening new pathways for us. It is left to us to find how to always be positive in looking at any circumstances. We are not supposed to become frustrated or to fall into despair, we are to be patient and keep moving forward, looking for other roads toward our happiness–which He has destined for us.

Furthermore, there is a blessing. The word 'blessing' is the translation of the Arabic word *baraka*. This word is closely related to the nature of God as the Merciful and the Compassionate. That is, when God gives goodness, He offers unlimited goodness. So *baraka* is usually translated as *ziyādat al-khayr* (addition or abundance of goodness). Not only are there visible advantages in every goodness, but they also come with the potential to remain with us for a long time.

Indeed, God has designed this universe such that it is teeming with goodness, unlimited in terms of the amount, type and timing. There is infinite goodness in this universe that permeates what is in it and sustains it from the beginning of creation until the end of time. None limits or cuts it off except man himself. It is man who, by his negative attitudes and viewpoints–failure to persevere, frustration, negative thinking about Divine creation, *kufr* (rejection) for His affection–causes the loss of this blessing upon himself.

That is why we should open our hearts to God's infinite goodness. Start with the positive frame of mind that goodness is always present in anything that comes to us. Be patient and grateful and goodness will accompany us always; it comes in many forms and continues to reside here with us.

Once we adopt this viewpoint, we will no longer see anything but good things in this universe. Not excluding calamities and disasters, they exist for the sake of goodness. Without the bad—or to be exact, what we think to be bad—the good will not be evident. Without the difficulty, or what we consider to be difficulty, what we know as ease will be obscured. Without sadness, how are joy and happiness to be born? This universe will not be materialized unless there is what we refer to as the bad. So, there is nothing left to say other than the 'bad' is the background upon which goodness is projected, becoming an integral part of the goodness, and therefore also becoming the realization of His compassion.

This is why the Prophet (peace be upon him) stated: 'If God loves a group of people, He will test them.'[1] That is, his humanity is tested with respect to his nobleness as a being that was created to emulate His sublime virtues. Only after he passes the test is he indeed ready to achieve all His goodness and *baraka*. Otherwise, or in the case he has not yet passed the test, then it is likely that he is still living in the animal stage, merely satisfying his own lust. Most likely he may be living a pleasant life, but he lacks concern for other human beings who may live in pain. His empathy is yet to be sharpened, his soul has yet to mature, and his life is still shallow. On top of all that, he has never really felt true happiness since he has never

1. Narrated by al-Tirmidhī.

lived in the opposite circumstances, in a place where happiness can be projected.

Let us try to 'enjoy' the ordeal, to learn to reach our maturity with Him. After all, He is also the Master Designer, He whose nature is love and compassion, He who has promised not to burden us with a test that we will not be able to bear.

The Order of Happiness[1] —Ibn Miskawayh

HAPPINESS, ACCORDING TO Aristotle, is divided into five components: Firstly, happiness of the body, which lies in such things as beauty, sensory acuity, good health and good temperament coming from a sound sense of hearing, sight, smell, taste and touch.

Secondly, happiness is found in the possession of fortune, friends and similar things on which one can spend his wealth anywhere he wants, and using such wealth to engage in good deeds, helping good people in particular and all eligible people in general. With wealth, one can engage in activities through which their nobleness can increase and for which they receive praise and applause.

Thirdly, happiness lies in a good name and renowned stature among noble people, because it means one has been recognized and appreciated for his attitude and good deeds.

1. Extracted from *Ibn Miskawayh* (Bandung: Mizan, 1999), pp. 92–104.

Fourthly, happiness is success in all respects. It is felt when one is able to realize perfectly their dreams and desires. Finally, the fifth happiness can only be obtained through becoming a man of conscientious understanding, appropriate thinking and undistorted beliefs. He is rarely wrong or tricked into error, both in terms of religious beliefs and nonreligious matters, and is able to provide proper guidance to others. According to Aristotle, if a man is filled with all these parts of happiness then he is a happy and perfect man. However, if he only reaches some parts he will only achieve happiness which corresponds to the level he has reached.

Earlier philosophers, such as Pythagoras, Socrates and Plato[2] postulated that virtue and happiness only belong to the soul. Therefore, when classifying happiness, they confined it to the capacity of the soul alone, namely wisdom, courage, modesty and justice, as we have mentioned at the beginning of this book. They also argued that those virtues are enough for happiness, and that people no longer need other virtues, either related to the body or outside the body; that if humans acquire such virtues, their happiness will not subside despite their illness or other physical ailments or disabilities. Happiness will only be disrupted by weak-mindedness and the like. Happiness will not be undermined by poverty, notoriety, lack of authoritative power and other flaws.

2. In two manuscripts which appear to be of the same group, it reads *wa-buqrat* (Hippocrates). In my reading, however, it reads *wa-saqrat* (Socrates), which is taken from, and in line with the views of Richard Walzer, *Greek into Arabic: Essays on Islamic Philosophy* (Cambridge, MA: Harvard University Press, 1962), p. 224, n. 3.

The Stoics and naturalists believe that the body is part of the human self. They did not regard the body as an instrument, as we have explained previously. Consequently, they considered the happiness of the soul as imperfect without happiness inside and outside the body, such as anything that can be obtained through good luck and fortune.

Reliable researchers, namely philosophers, excluded good luck and everything that is obtained through good luck. They do not include these things in the category of happiness, because happiness is seen as something fixed, indestructible and unchangeable. Happiness is the noblest, the highest, and the most honourable thing. They argue that the lowest things—which are ever-changing, unfixed and not borne in ideas or virtues—cannot take part in happiness.

Can Happiness be Cultivated in the World?

It is for this reason that classical thinkers disagree on the level of peak happiness. Some of them assume that the pinnacle of happiness cannot be attained by humans before they part from their bodies and all physical things. It is this group, which we have previously observed, who suggest that the pinnacle of happiness is in the soul. They confine human attributes to substance alone, excluding the body. Therefore, they conclude that as long as the soul is still inhabiting the body which is stained with dust, dirt, self-importance and bodily needs, the soul is not really happy. They see that the soul has not yet reached the perfection associated with the existence of all things intellectual, because these things are unknown to us due to the darkness of our matter. Based on this, they assume that if the soul has been separated from this turbidity, meaning it has parted from ignorance, it becomes clean, pure and ready to receive divine light, namely the Perfect Intellect. Perceived from this very view, humans will never be really happy, except in the Hereafter.

Another group say that it is a real shame to consider that a man who during his life was capable of doing good deeds, believed in the right principles, strived to acquire blessings both for himself and for his family and assumed his role as a good caliph of God by conducting all things with which God is pleased; it is a shame to consider this man to be on the same footing as a man who lived in suffering and deprivation–and then, just because he died, he had no more to do with all the problems above. Rather, the latter should not be considered to be perfectly happy and prosperous.

Aristotle agrees with this view, as is apparent in his discussion about human happiness. According to him, man is composed of body and soul. It is therefore natural that he defines man as a rational creature who could die, or as a two-footed rational creature, along with other definitions. This group of thought led by Aristotle argue that in this world people can attain peak happiness and welfare provided that they are willing to work hard to achieve it.

Aristotle recognizes and sets forth the proposition that happiness is also different between humans, and that this is a severe problem for them. The philosopher explains and discusses this in depth. The poor perceive that the greatest happiness lies in the wealth and ease of life; the sick think happiness lies in good health and wellbeing; those who are feeling despised, think happiness lies in glory and power; the evil see happiness in fulfilment of their varied lusts and desires; people who fall in love believe happiness lies in winning their beloved's heart, and the noble and honourable see that happiness lies in doing good for deserving people. Some philosophers suggest that all of the categories of happiness mentioned above are different once we arrange them according to the needs of the mind, for happiness is to be sought when needed–at the right time and in the right way. They also believe that what is desirable for the sake of something else is less worthy than something called 'happiness'.

Since each of these two groups have equally voiced their views on happiness, here we are obliged to express our opinions on what we deem as correct, while also summarizing the two earlier opinions.

The Author's View of Happiness

Human beings have a spiritual gift with which they can emulate the good spirits, often called angels. We also have a physical element, which makes us similar to animals. This is because man is composed of these two components. Armed with the physical, with which he can match the animals, man lives in this 'low-realm' for a relatively short period, to govern and bring prosperity to the Earth. As soon as he has managed to achieve perfection in carrying out his degree of humanity, he will move into the 'high-realm', to eternally and peacefully reside with the angels or good spirits. But first, we must understand what the low and high realms are.

As we have pointed out, the high-realm is not a high place perceived by the senses nor is the low-realm a low place perceived by the senses. Anything that can be reached by the senses is part of the lower-realm, even though it is located on high ground, and anything that becomes the object of the mind is of the high-realm, although it is located in a low place. There is one more thing that we all should know. Namely, bodily happiness is no longer needed among spirits who have separated themselves from the body. Instead, they need happiness of the soul, namely wisdom, which is an eternal object of the mind. So, as long as man is still man, his happiness is incomplete unless both conditions are achieved together and these two conditions cannot be obtained, except by means of a medium that brings him to eternal wisdom. Then, a happy man definitely lives in one of two levels: (1) he stays at the level of the physical realm, embraces his low circumstances and is happy in them. Along with that he looks for noble things, strives to earn precious things, loves them and is satisfied with them; or (2) he belongs to the level of the spiritual realm, adheres to higher causes and is happy in them. He observes and examines low things, takes lessons from them, contemplates the signs of divine power and the proofs of perfect wisdom, follows their example, organizes and conveys goodness and uses them as a guide to obtaining a chain of virtues.

He who has not reached one of the two levels is still suited to the animal level, or even lower, because this level is closed to the goodness of the higher level, and is not endowed with the ability to climb higher. Instead, its own characteristic only allows it to move towards the perfections that correspond to its level. This differentiates animal from man; man can be invited to achieve higher levels and is equipped for achieving them.

Unfortunately, he is often carried away by distractions and fails to obtain higher levels, or does not attempt to attain them. He prefers things the other way and uses his noble potential to gain lowly things. Animals, on the contrary, reach a perfection of their own. It is forgivable that animals do not perform humanly virtues, and consequently they do not have the opportunity to join the spirits and to enter the Paradise that was promised to righteous people. As for human beings, it is inexcusable. The former is exactly like a blind man who deviates from the path and plunges into a well. Here we should pity him, but he is not wrong. The latter is similar to a good-sighted man who walks but also falls into a well. He is culpable and does not need to be pitied.

Thus, it is clear that happy people must be at one of the two levels we have mentioned. It is also clear that a certain type of happy person is imperfect and inadequate for others. Being imperfect means he is not free from suffering, because he has been deceived by the enticements of the desires that deter him from his goal and keep him busy with worldly affairs. People of this level are not completely perfect, nor really happy. Only people who have reached the next level will be completely happy. They have a lot of wisdom and, equipped with their spirituality, they are among those high creatures from whom they may gain yet more wisdom. They acquire a divine radiance and seek to increase their virtues up to the limit of their abilities. Therefore, they will forever be free from the misery which binds people of the first level. They will live happily in themselves forever, in their own condition and within the divine radiance they constantly receive. They will be happy with these things alone; they will be happy only with beauty. They are happy only when they see the wisdom of the wise. Their soul will not be peaceful, except when they stick to their own kind or whoever is close to their kind, from whom they want to learn. Once someone manages to reach this level, he reaches the pinnacle of happiness. He is a person who does not mind parting with his beloved in the world, he is a person who does not grieve for not receiving worldly pleasures, and he is one who views the body, wealth and all worldly pleasures–which we have mentioned above as happiness inside and outside the body–as nothing more than a burden, consumed merely to the extent required by the body from where he cannot be separated unless that is what the Creator wills.

He's a person who longs to be with the community of his kind, to gather with other good spirits and chosen angels; he is a person who will not do anything unless God wills, who opts for something that would bring him to Him. He will not disobey Him by following his lowly desires, nor will he be deceived by lust, nor will he be distracted by something in his way towards happiness. He will not grieve over a loss of something that he loves, nor will he live in sorrow after failing to fulfil his desire.

However, this last stage is the level in which people greatly vary, meaning this level is reached by people from many different classes. These two levels are what the philosopher, Aristotle discusses in his book *Virtues of the Soul (Faḍā'il al-Nafs),* and he prefers the latter.

Pleasure in this Happiness the Only True Pleasure

He who both knows the essence of this happiness and knows how to express it in his behaviour is someone who enjoys happiness and real joy. He transcends love towards ecstasy (*'ishq*) and bliss. At such times he will not let high motives within him be subdued by low-bodily motives. From this point on, he is no longer a slave to his lower soul because his noble soul is no longer subdued by the lower one.

By pleasure that is stained with falsehood, I mean the pleasures of ours and non-rational animals. These pleasures are linked to our desire, are short in duration and quickly dull our senses. The longer the pleasures last, the duller our senses will be, and pleasure can even turn into pain. Our senses have a particular accidental (nonessential) pleasure, unlike our minds. Our mind's pleasure is essential, whereas pleasures of the senses are just accidental.

For that reason, he who does not know the essential pleasure will not enjoy true pleasure. Whoever does not recognize the cause of the essential (happiness), is not likely to crave it. We have often discussed this matter and we have frequently recommended this to be worthy of our attention. We have even stated that those who do not recognize the absolute goodness, the perfect virtue, and do not learn practical wisdom, that is prioritizing the best, practising it and being steadfast in it, will surely not enjoy it. And whoever knows the essential pleasure will feel the joy of goodness that we are describing.

A Happy Man's Attitude towards Ill Fortune

You should know that as long as happy people, whose condition we have explained earlier, are alive in this universe—that persists with all its planets and stars and with its good and bad luck—they will be struck by calamities and misfortunes which also befall other kinds of people. The difference is, happy people will not be afraid, nor will they encounter the difficulties as other people will. They will not be immediately affected because they are not accustomed to fear or grief. They are also unaffected by difficulties and bitterness caused by accidental conditions. Even if pain befalls them they will be able to restrain themselves, so they will stay happy. They are not going to be dragged out of the realm of happiness at all, even though they may be tested like that of the Prophet Job (Ayyūb) or more than that, they will remain strong. This could happen because they possess the required courage and patience to face what is scary for servants with a weak character. So, they are content with themselves and earn a blessing for their goodness. They know how killers who show their ferocity, or a wrestler who craves for victory, must suppress their desires and withstand great suffering, in order to obtain victory and a good name. They think it reasonable and appropriate for them to be patient, because their goal is nobler and their good name among the virtuous is far greater, more honorable and respectable; and because they have reached the happiness of the soul and have become the role model for others.

Aristotle says, 'Most effects of bad luck are trivial and easy to deal with.' So, merely being able to accept bad luck doesn't make a man prove the limit of his spirit and the strength of his determination. He who has never been happy or traversed the noble way of moral purification, when bad luck befalls him. will be in one of two conditions: either deeply affected and suffering so that people feel sorry for him; or searching for happy people and listening to their advice, so that he can exhibit patience and a peaceful attitude, although in fact he is still agitated, fearful and suffering.

Just as a part of the body suffering palsy or paralysis will move to the right when the left is intended, so the soul of the vile does the same; it moves away from goodness when it is directed to go there. When bad people follow those who are good and just, their souls move in the opposite direction, no matter how they propel their souls toward the good.

Pleasure in Happiness is Active, Essential and Complete

After we have established that happiness is something that brings the greatest pleasure, and is the paramount and utmost good, we must now demonstrate, in a more complete fashion than before, the aspects of pleasure within happiness. Pleasure is of two kinds, one passive the other active. Passive pleasure is shared by humans as well as non-rational animals, it being passive as it is the result of the intense stimulation of some desire or impulse, or a requited fondness, all of which moves two animal souls. Active pleasure is peculiar to the rational soul. Neither being material, nor being subject to involuntary incitement, its pleasure is pure and essential, while that of the first one is impure and accidental.

What we mean by essential and accidental is that carnal pleasures as a result of lust are temporary, short-lived and are liable to get transformed into misery or something that is repugnant. When that happens, it is an example of the opposite, something that is opposed to pleasure. On the other hand, essential pleasure can never ever become its opposite. Its state will not change and hence will always remain constant. If this is the case, then what we have stated is both true and lucid: the pleasure that brings one happiness is essential not accidental, intellectual not carnal, active not passive, divine not animal.

That is why philosophers have said that pleasure, whenever it is genuine, can guide the body from deficiency towards perfection and from sickness towards health. Similarly, it will guide the soul from ignorance towards knowledge, from debasement towards virtue. However, this pleasure is a hidden secret. A seeker is strongly advised to uncover it. It must be emphasized however that people are strongly drawn towards carnal pleasures, and though our desire to enjoy them is problematic, it is difficult to weaken this carnal desire, as it has been with us since our original inception. It is for this reason that when these bodily pleasures are sinful, when people incline too far towards the lower desires and are thus overwhelmed by them, humans start to consider good all that is vile, thinking nothing of sins however obscene. They are then unable to see wrongs and iniquitous deeds for what they are, unless they are enlightened by divine wisdom.

Quite contrary to the above are good intellectual pleasures. However, human nature does not immediately take to these and thus, when someone wishes to approach them to gain knowledge and appreciation of this realm, they need patience and labour. Once one has contemplated and practiced conscientiously, only then can one realize the beauty of these intellectual pleasures, and award them their deserving place. It is thus clear that from the very outset of the process of human growth and development, one needs to be guided, whether by parents, by divine guidance, or by the correct religion, so that one is able to rejuvenate oneself to steer towards pure enlightenment and towards the goal of one's life.

The relationship between happiness and generosity is also evident, as we have mentioned earlier. Happiness is the pleasure of a knower, and the happiness of one who does good deeds lies in giving, while the pleasure of one who receives lies in receiving. The pleasure of a happy person lies in doing virtuous deeds, and manifesting gnosis, placing it in the place that it deserves. An artisan will be happy if he is able to demonstrate his artistic ability and exhibit his art in front of admirers. This is the true meaning and the reality of generosity. It must be remembered that to be generous in the highest and most noble endeavors is far more honorable and superior to being generous in lesser and ordinary things. This generosity of the first order, with noble and lofty stature, is the opposite of the second one, which is insignificant. This is so because the fortune of a wealthy person decreases when expended or given to others, whereas the fortune of the possessor of true happiness will never decrease despite his freely giving it away, rather it will increase. A wealthy person may encounter threats in the form of enemies, thieves and robbers, whereas a possessor of happiness is guarded against all such threats and perils, as there is no way for a criminal to seize this wealth no matter what strategies they apply.

7

Being Grateful and Patient in Facing Trials

THERE WAS ONCE a worker who was working on a multi-storey construction project. One day, he received a call on his mobile phone informing him that his co-worker's child was ill, and that the father needed to rush home. His co-worker's family had been forced to convey the news through him since his co-worker's mobile phone was not active. Unfortunately, he was working on a higher floor while the father of the sick child was on the ground floor. He wondered how to pass the message at such a distance, since his colleague wasn't even looking up at him. He had a spur of the moment idea to drop a coin on top of his co-worker's construction hat to grab his attention. The coin falling on the hat startled the co-worker, but instead of looking up he simply picked up the fallen coin and pocketed it. 'Not bad,' he thought, resuming his work. From above, the concerned worker kept on tossing coins until there were no coins left in his pocket. As he had run out of coins, the worker grabbed a handful of gravel and flung it down. The gravel landed right on his co-worker's hat and discovering that he was struck by gravel, the upset co-worker looked up. Only then was he able to hear his friend yelling from above him, telling him the news. Sometimes, good things come in unpleasant packaging.

***

Life is not a bed of roses. In fact, God states in the Qur'an that: 'Life and death were created to test you (and see) who among you is best in deed.' (*al-Mulk* 67:2) The Prophet reinforced this by stating: 'If Allah loves a group of people, He will test them,' and it is even reported that on one occasion he asserted that he 'would not eat or drink from the cup that belongs to someone who is not known to have been tested by God.' The test is in the form of difficulty or a challenge. The difficulty, as stated in the Qur'an, could take the form of death (of loved ones) or paucity of resources. In fact, Allah will surely test those who call themselves believers, as He tried those who came before us. They were shaken (by tribulations) so hard that they beseeched: 'When will God's help come?' (Although it should always be borne in mind that God has guaranteed that He would not burden his servants with anything they could not bear).

In fact, more and more people live in this world, submerging themselves into a state of pursuing the satisfaction of their base desires, thereby turning into the negligent (*ghāfil*). Their life is driven, nay subjugated, by desires rather than by their pure innate nature (*fiṭrah*). Desires that become accustomed to being satisfied and gratified, which not only makes them addicted and subservient but also makes them vulnerable to becoming disheartened each time anything they desire is not realized. Not only that, since our innate nature always looks for perfection and spiritual peace, carnal satisfaction could never usher in true happiness for us. Instead, we are at great risk of tremendous chagrin, desolation and bewilderment once we discover that we had all that we desired but still we failed to achieve the happiness we expected. So, where else should we seek happiness? From this point, we are expected to better understand the purpose of our life, the source of our life and also our true identity (*fiṭrah*), then organize our lives in accordance with them. This is actually what guarantees our happiness, not just in the afterlife—where our deeds are rewarded—but also in this world. Because no matter how well we gratify our desires, we will never be able to make our lives happy, nay, the opposite will take place.

All the trials of this life are intended to challenge us to be introspective, to dig deeper into our souls—rather than allow ourselves to remain living superficially on the shallow surface—in search of the meaning of life. Through trials, we can expect to improve the quality of our life from one that is actually animalistic—only satisfying physical needs—to a more human life. In other words, man who is endowed with a mind and a heart, who is granted with an innate nature to be kind, who is assigned to be His caliph, should serve as an agent of love and kindness in this world.

It is worth noting that trials (*balā'*) from Allah do not always come in the form of difficulty. His gifts could also be a test. Wealth, for example, could become a source of arrogance if we fail to see them as God's gift entrusted to us, for the sake of ourselves and of others in need of our help. So could intelligence, power and popularity.

A further analysis will show us that we are taught to be patient even when accepting a gift. We are taught to prevent the gift from clouding our mind and turning into disaster, both for ourselves and for others. And by contrast, we are taught to be grateful in dealing with difficulties, realizing that everything comes from God. So, not only do we believe that we must accept them willingly, we must also be sure that they will actually strengthen our faith.

Indeed, patience and gratitude are two sides of the same coin. He who is able to be grateful is at the same time a person who is able to be patient, and vice versa. They are the kind of people that will always receive an outpouring of gifts (*wa-la-in-shakartum lāzīdannakum*). More than that, they are the ones who are truly happy:

> *Give good tidings to the patient, who, when calamity befalls them say, 'Innā li-Llāhi wa-innā ilayhi rāji'ūn' (Indeed we belong to Allah, and indeed to Him we will return).* (*al-Baqarah* 2: 155–156)

8

Actualizing Noble Character Traits

CALIPH 'UMAR B. 'ABD AL-'AZĪZ once approached a shepherd boy who was herding goats belonging to his employer. The Caliph learned that the young man was herding dozens of goats, and he wanted to test the young boy's honesty. He said, 'Hey, boy, would you sell the goats to me?' The young man replied, 'They are not mine; they belong to my master.'

'But,' said Caliph 'Umar, 'if you sell just one, surely your master will not know.'

The young man looked up at the Caliph and said, 'My master might not know, but Allah would.'

***

The Prophet (peace be upon him) once stated that: 'Virtue is what brings peace to your mind, and vice is what troubles your heart.' Indeed, tranquillity and inner peace can only be achieved by people who have integrity. The word 'integrity' comes from 'integer' which means a round number that is not a fraction. The general meaning of integrity is fidelity to morality, without which one cannot enjoy a life that is full, tranquil or happy (fulfilled). Its essence is uniformity between words and deeds, and harmony between a person's moral values and their actual deeds. People who have integrity will have noble character because they are convinced of the virtues of noble character. Whereas those who do not have integrity will in reality have a base character, contrary to the impression they give people.

People who lack this kind of integrity will naturally develop a split personality. In the Holy Qur'an, God states: 'Most loathsome is it in the sight of God that you say what you do not do!' (*al-saff* 61:3) If we see Paradise as gaining Allah's pleasure (*riḍwān*), then indeed the wrath of God corresponds to Hell or misery in life.

In Islamic terminology, it is safe to say that possessing integrity is similar to having good or praiseworthy character (*al-akhlāq al-karīmah*). The linguistic meaning of *akhlāq* (or its singular form *khuluq*) itself hints at a fundamental aspect of it. Sharing the same root with *khalq* (creation) *khāliq* (creator) and *makhlūq* (creature), the word *akhlāq* or *khuluq* refers to Islam's basic view that man—as 'the best of creation' (*aḥsan taqwīm*)—was created in (or with a tendency towards) goodness, purity and dignity. So, as we have mentioned before, people of integrity are actually those whose deeds are good, or in accordance with his or her belief in the goodness of humanity's *fiṭrah*.

The role of character is of such importance in Islam that the Prophet Muhammad summarized his whole prophetic task as perfecting human character: 'I have not been sent except to perfect noble character.'[1]

In another hadith, he even taught: 'What brings the most people into Paradise are *taqwā* (being ever conscious of God, which gives rise to noble character) and good deeds.'[2] Hence, one cannot truly be a believer unless he assumes a good character. The Prophet said: 'The best among you are those who have the best character.'[3] In fact it is difficult to separate faith from noble character. Thus, there is no faith that can be legitimately accepted by Allah unless manifested in noble character.

Akhlāq is concerned with individual and social behavior. Individual *akhlāq* means a clean heart full of love and affection; for God, for fellow human beings and for all the inhabitants of the universe. While social *akhlāq* means good deeds, such as all efforts to improve one's surroundings, including overcoming poverty and oppression, improving the quality of people's educational opportunities, preventing environmental destruction and curbing despondency.

From the brief description above, it is obvious that not only is our happiness in the Hereafter at stake in our good character, both as individuals and as members of society, but our happiness in this world is also completely dependent on it. People who have a good character, namely those who have absolute integrity, are complete humans who live their lives to the full; and only a complete human can live in balance and stability, in peace and happiness

1. Narrated by Malik and Ahmad.
2. Narrated by al-Tirmidhī.
3. Narrated by al-Bukhari and Muslim.

9

Spreading Righteous Deeds

ONCE, IN THE midst of a journey, Shaqīq al-Balkhī, travelling with his teacher Ibrāhīm b. Adham, found a bird on the ground fluttering with a broken wing. Before the two men could help, in flew another bird and started feeding the bird with the broken wing. Shaqīq, as if to himself, said: 'Why am I worried about my provision when God has guaranteed the sustenance even of a bird whose wing is broken.' Hearing that, Ibrāhīm ibn Adham said: 'How strange of you, Shaqīq, to only heed the broken winged bird instead of heeding the healthy bird that is feeding those in need?' By that the teacher implied that doing the best with what we have is far better than resigning ourselves to fate.

***

God created life for us to flood it with righteous deeds. These good deeds would serve as capital invested for the fulfilment of our hopes to be able to see Him.

> *So whoever hopes to meet with his Lord, let him do righteous deeds ...* (*al-Kahf* 18: 110).

The word 'righteous' (*ṣāliḥ*) comes from the word *ṣalāḥ* which means good, useful or healthy. This word is repeated 180 times in the Qur'an. Righteous deeds can be defined as any action that provides benefits, eliminates difficulties and brings about improvements. More than simply being righteous, a pious person always works hard, spending their time wisely, contributing to society, making a difference in people's lives. This concept is of such importance that, among 180 verses in the Qur'an containing this word, Allah frequently associates it with faith itself, in the same breath.

> *Whoever does righteous works, whether male or female, while he is a believer, We will surely cause him to live a good life* (*ḥayāh ṭayyibah*). (*al-Naḥl* 16: 97)

The above verse clearly teaches us that God will bestow happiness, not only in Paradise, but in this world also—especially for people who perform righteous acts. A guaranteed happiness for people who do righteous deeds is expressed once again in a different verse, as follows:

> *[and so it is that] they who attain to faith and do righteous deeds are destined for happiness [in this world] and the most beauteous of all goals [in the life to come].* (*al-Ra'd* 13: 29)

Elsewhere in the Qur'an, Allah says:

> *Wealth and children are an adornment of this world's life: but good deeds, the fruit whereof endures forever (al-bāqiyāt al-ṣāliḥāt), are of far greater merit in thy Sustainer's sight, and a far better source of hope.* (*al-Kahf* 18: 46)

According to some commentators, the term *al-bāqiyāt al-ṣāliḥāt* can also be interpreted as (a source of) happiness.

Meanwhile, in *Sūrah al-'Aṣr* Allah states that those who believe and do good, and advise each other about truth and patience, are excluded from loss:

> *By time. Indeed man is in loss, except for those who have believed and done righteous works; and advised each other to truth; and advised each other to patience.* (*al-'Aṣr* 103: 1–3)

Some interpretations convey that by associating good deeds with time, God intended to command us to fill our lives with as many good deeds as possible. In this respect, the Prophet (peace be upon him) is reported to have said: 'A believer does not stop keeping busy (in doing righteous works) right until his last breath.'[1]

Obviously this is in line with what was said by Allah in the Qur'an: 'So when you have finished [your duties], then stand up [for worship] and to your Lord direct [your] longing.' (*al-Sharḥ* 94: 7–8)

1. Narrated by Aḥmad and al-Bazzār.

In fact, this is precisely what was taught by the Prophet (peace be upon him) throughout his life, which he dedicated wholeheartedly to the improvement of society, the elimination of difficulties and the benefit of humankind.

So, let us fill our lives with righteous deeds in the hope that God would bless our lives in this world and in the Hereafter and that He would grant us true happiness.

10

Subduing Egoism

ONCE THE FOLLOWERS of Prophet Mūsā (peace be upon him) requested that the prophet ask God to come to see them. Due to the insistence of his people, Mūsā prayed to God to grant the request. God agreed. He asked Mūsā to take his people to a cave and wait there. Three days passed and Mūsā and his people anxiously waited. However, God did not appear. So, once again, urged by his people, Mūsā prayed to God: 'O God, you promised to come, but three days have passed, and you have not come.'

God said: 'Indeed, I came to you three times on three consecutive days. The first day, someone came to you who was hungry and you did not feed him. That was Me.' Then God said: 'The second day, someone came to you who was thirsty and you did not give him to drink. That was Me. The third day, someone came to you as a runaway and you did not accept him. That was Me.'

***

What brings us closer to God? The answer is freedom from egoism. Conversely, the more we inflate our ego, the further we will move away from Allah. This is what may be known as *shirk*, or treating one's self (interest) as God.

Indeed, Allah is in our heart and He resides in every human heart. However, we repeatedly cover His presence with our indulgence in lust and ego. As a result, our access to Allah is impeded, so that His presence has no impact on the quality of our lives.

Allah states in the Qur'an that He did not create two hearts inside the human bosom. Rather, He created one heart (*al-Aḥzāb* 33: 4). What this means is that filling our only heart with worldly things or indulging ourselves in selfishness leaves no space inside for Allah. Worse than that, egoism is the root of the diseases of the heart (pride, envy, backbiting and miserliness) that will break the link between humans and their *Khāliq* (the Creator). No wonder the Sufis say that the peak of one's relationship with Allah is reached when one attains *fanā'* (annihilation in God). *Fanā'* occurs when man is able to conquer his selfhood/ego and selfishness, which then allows him to go back to Allah, The Origin.

How to Overcome Egoism?

The enemies of egoism are sacrifice and giving. Giving means taking from what we have and handing it over to others. Giving means to reduce our supply of indulgence in passion. Islam insists that we will not achieve goodness unless we donate or give. It is said in the Qur'an when describing the characteristics of the pious: '*wa-āta al-māl 'alā ḥubbihi*' 'and they give from their wealth despite their love for it', rather than simply sharing a little from the excess wealth they possess. And it must be done with sincerity, merely for the sake of goodness and a desire for His pleasure. In fact, if we find miserliness in our hearts (entertaining the thought of hoarding instead of giving), it means we have not reached the stage of 'giving what we love'.

Similarly, as was recorded in the Qur'an when the Prophet (peace be upon him) was asked: '*Mādhā yunfiqūn?*' 'What must they spend [in the way of Allah]?', Allah instructed the Prophet to say, '*al-'afw*', which means whatever remains after our needs are fulfilled. All the wealth exceeding our needs should be given to someone in need.

The Qur'an portrays a good Muslim as a man who has the spirit of altruism (*īthār*), namely putting others above ourselves.

That is why, in the Qur'an Allah always mentions prayers and giving in the same breath. Prayers, despite being called the most important form of worship, are meaningless if not followed by acts of giving. In a deeper perspective, prayers are classified as void if they do not provide positive social impact.

This spirit of sacrifice is beautifully reflected by the Prophet Ibrāhīm (peace be upon him). Imagine, as is recorded in an account, that he had turned eighty and still had no children. Then, after he had a child, Allah ordered him to sacrifice that dear child for whom he had been yearning for so long. Ibrāhīm carried out the order without hesitation; he did it with full surrender. Is there any greater sacrifice than that? With that, the sacrifice of the Prophet Ibrāhīm is an example of a *ḥanīf,* a man who has the desire to unite with Allah.

Ibrāhīm has proven himself not only to be a practitioner of monotheism in the literal sense, but also achieving a high degree of *taqwā*. Concerning this sacrificial worship, the Qur'an states: 'Their meat will not reach Allah, nor will their blood.' (*al-Ḥajj* 22: 37) What reaches Him is our *taqwā* (piety). Piety is most appropriately translated as: our awareness of Allah; that wherever we are we always strive to do what pleases Him.

Man is indeed a spark of the spirit of God, wrapped in flesh and blood. The Prophet's teachings encapsulate the idea that God is love; and the nature of love is the spirit of giving and sacrifice. Thus, man's innate nature is to give. His happiness lies in his conformity with his giving nature. Otherwise, his *fiṭrah* will suffer and happiness will elude him. Conversely, giving will guarantee happiness in our lives.

In conclusion, maintaining our closeness to Allah is the practical way to live happily in this world, in *barzakh* (the realm between death and Resurrection) and in the Hereafter. By preserving our nearness to God, we will live a happy life in this world, a happier life in *barzakh* and the happiest life in the Hereafter. And the only way to achieve closeness to our Beloved, Allah, is by giving to and sacrificing for the sake of those who need our helping hand.

11

Happiness as Freedom from Hate

ANAS IBN MĀLIK reported: We were sitting with the Messenger of Allah, peace be upon him, and he said, 'Coming upon you now is a man from the people of Paradise.' A man from the Ansar came whose beard was disheveled by the water of ablution and he was carrying both of his shoes with his left hand. The next day the Prophet repeated the same words, and the man came in the same condition. The third day the Prophet repeated the same again, and the man came in the same condition. When the Prophet stood up to leave, 'Abdullāh ibn 'Amr followed the man and he said, 'I am in a dispute with my father and I have sworn not to enter my home for three days. May I stay with you?' The man said yes.

'Abdullāh stayed three nights with the man but he never saw him praying at night. Whenever he went to bed, he would remember Allah and rest until he woke up for morning prayer. Abdullah said that he never heard anything but good words from his mouth. When three nights had passed and he did not see anything special about his actions, 'Abdullāh asked him, 'O servant of

Allah, I have not been in dispute with my father nor have I cut relations with him. I heard the Prophet say three times that a man from the people of Paradise was coming to us and then you came. I thought I should stay with you to see what you are doing that I should follow, but I did not see you do anything special. Why did the Prophet speak highly of you?' The man said, 'I am as you have seen.' When Abdullah was about to leave, the man said, 'I am as you have seen, except that I do not find hatred and ill-intentions (*ghish*) in my soul towards the Muslims (in another version, 'people') and I do not envy anyone because of the good that Allah has bestowed upon them.' Abdullah said, 'This is what you have achieved and it is something we have not accomplished.'[1]

The narration in al-Bazzār identifies this person as Sa'd, and his last statement is :

> *There are no (deeds) other than those you have seen, O son of my brother, except that I do not sleep in a state of hate (ḍagīna), in other versions malice (ghill) towards a Muslim (or people).*[2]

Anas ibn Mālik reported that the Messenger of Allah (peace be upon him) said to me: O boy, if you are able every morning and evening to remove any rancor from your heart towards anyone, then do so. Then the Prophet (peace be upon him) said:

1. There is difference of opinion as to the authenticity of this hadith. Some hadith scholars deem it soundly transmitted, while others do not. However, many lessons may be drawn from it.
2. Narrated by Aḥmad and al-Bazzār

> *O boy, that is my tradition (sunnah) and whoever revives my tradition has loved me, and whoever loves me will be with me in Paradise.*[3]

If there is one thing, we are sure, that should not be present in a Muslim, it is to possess, or hold a grudge or hatred towards anyone. Even against those who are not Muslims. Indeed, as can be seen in the example of the debate of Prophet Ibrāhīm (peace be upon him) with those who disbelieved from his people, Allah taught him to say:

> *Verily, we are quit of you and of all that you worship instead of God: we deny the truth of whatever you believe; and between us and you there has arisen enmity and hatred, to last until such a time as you come to believe in the One God!* (*Al-Mumtahanah* 60:4)

We can see that while referring to the declaration of enmity/hostility towards the disbelievers by the Prophet Ibrahim (peace be upon him), the Quran uses the word '*abadan*', which means 'forever'. Even so, he restricts it using the phrase, 'until you come to believe in the One God'. What does that indicate? Without doubt, what is disliked/hated, is the lack of belief, not the people themselves. It is highlighted that hatred or enmity is a temporary state, and is removed without a trace as soon as they attain to a state of belief.

3. Narrated by al-Tirmidhī

The imperative to be free from this hatred can be explained in another way. It is the duty of all Muslims to invite others towards good/Islam. Well, how will we be motivated to invite others towards good, if we hate them? What will happen instead, is the exact opposite. If we hate someone, we would end up wishing misfortune for them, punishment in this world and even hellfire.

It means that the foundational prerequisite of preaching to someone is that we do not hate those whom we may consider to be in error.

Indeed, it is in this context that God characterized the noble Prophet (peace be upon him) using the following words:

> *And it was by God's grace that you [O Prophet] dealt gently with your followers: for if you had been harsh and hard of heart, they would indeed have broken away from you.* (*Al-Imran* 3:159)

Learning from the example of the Prophet (peace be upon him), love, affection and freedom from hatred and malice must be an ingrained character of all those who seek to invite others towards good.

Not just that, freedom from hatred and malice will make us gracious people, and make our life in this world peaceful and happy. Whether it is to attain paradise in this world, or to achieve the character of the inhabitants of the Paradise of the next world, as stated in the Quran: And [by then] We shall have removed any hatred/envy (ghill) that may have been [lingering] in their breasts, [and they shall rest] as brethren, facing one another [in love] upon thrones of happiness. (*al-Ḥijr* 15:47)

And so, they who come after them pray: '*O our Sustainer! Forgive us our sins, as well as those of our brethren who preceded us in faith, and let not our hearts entertain any unworthy thoughts or feelings against [any of] those who have attained to faith. O our Sustainer! Verily, You are Compassionate, the Dispenser of Grace!*' (*al-Ḥashr* 59:10)

12

Overcoming Our Addiction to Wealth

IBRĀHĪM B. ADHAM, a Sufi, used to be a ruler in Balkh before giving up all his worldly privileges. He once met a man who wanted to give him some money. Ibrāhīm said: 'If you are rich, I will accept your gift. But if you are needy, I will not.' The man then tried to give assurances regarding his affluence and prosperity resulting in the following conversation:

Ibrāhīm responded: 'How much money have you got?'

Man: 'I have five thousand pieces of gold.'

Ibrāhīm: 'Do you want to have ten thousand pieces of gold?'

Man: 'Yes, of course.'

Ibrāhīm : 'Are you going to be happier if you have twenty thousand pieces of gold?'

Man: 'Yes, that is certainly better.'

Ibrāhīm : 'Then you're not rich at all! You're more in need of this money than I am. I am satisfied with whatever He gives me. I cannot receive anything from someone whose expectations are insatiable.'

***

Lately we are experiencing how obsessed our lives have become with wealth and belongings. How avarice drives us to chase possessions, for which we must pay dearly in many forms, such as with the loss of awareness of our humanity, the obscuring of our understanding regarding the purpose of life and creation, as well as a distorted perspective regarding paths to happiness.

As a result, many modern human beings–especially those living in big cities–no longer live as humans. 'Zombies' would be a more befitting term to use for them, the undead creatures who mindlessly roam about without any sense of self-awareness. A lacking of perspective about how to achieve happiness has sent us head over heels in our search for money to buy things; rushing to and fro, being unconcerned about time and neglecting our family and other people. Whereas, if we reflect, we become conscious of the fact that the essence of our humanity lies in our spirit and in our consciousness, rather than in our physical reality. We will come to realize that we were not created by Allah to be on this earth without purpose, but instead for a serious purpose: to do our utmost to worship Him. Foremost in this regard is: the necessity to cultivate *ṣilat al-raḥim* (maintaining kind and loving relationships), doing as many good deeds as possible for others and improving the quality of life of those around us.

Unfortunately, what is actually happening is the exact opposite. Through an assortment of media, that permeates every aspect of our lives, we are enticed to hanker after artificial needs, superfluous 'needs' that do not serve any function in making our lives happier. Prior to the ascent and ascendancy of modernity and the industrial era, people worked with a clear objective: to achieve wellbeing. Germane to this, wealth and possessions were deemed as a means to an end, not as an end itself. By that account, for all practical purposes, men lived more as 'human beings' in the past than they do today. Granted that science and technology have advanced by leaps and bounds in the present day, it seems obvious that people in the past seemed to be more skilled at managing their lives and maintaining their perspective regarding their work and business. In other words, they were better at their efforts in the pursuit of happiness than their counterparts today. Many of us nowadays end up sacrificing happiness in the pursuit of money. The clear distinction between 'purpose' and 'means' of life is obscured. As a testament to this, time and again we witness people becoming stranded in a life bereft of meaning, even after having obtained all the money that they were after. It turns out that hoarding wealth aplenty does not bring happiness nor meaning in life.

So then the question is, what is the correct way to make sense of money?

First of all, religion is neither opposed to anyone endeavouring to seek money, nor to anyone's effort in seeking Allah's blessings. As mentioned earlier, in the Qur'an Allah says: 'Seek instead, by means of what God has granted you, [the good of] the life to come, without forgetting your [rightful] share in this world.' (*al-Qaṣaṣ* 28: 77) It is important, however, that we continually foster the correct perspective concerning the possession of money and wealth. That money, once again, is a *means*, not the objective of our life. With such an undistorted outlook, no one would want to sacrifice their happiness–

the goal of their life—for the pursuit of money. Money should be subservient to our efforts to achieve a happy life.

Secondly, we need to rectify our priorities—that our life's duty is to worship Him, by way of spreading His blessings to the entire universe. As a matter of fact, our happiness lies here. Man was created by God with an innate nature to love. One will be unable to reach happiness and satisfaction without loving and manifesting that nature of love by doing good to others. Money, or our possessions, are merely a means to support us in our efforts to do the same.

Thirdly, we need to build and foster an awareness that our happiness in the world and in the Hereafter does not lie in the amount of money and possessions we have. Rather, it lies in how we perceive its functions and in the way we utilize it. So, with gratitude, expend it for lawful and worthy things; abstain from a profligate lifestyle and use your surplus wealth for the sake of others. Only then will you achieve happiness, both in this world and the next.

Never let money be like the proverbial touch of Midas, whose golden touch turned even his own daughter into gold, thus becoming a cause of great unhappiness rather than a boon. Never let money, which is supposed to assist us in achieving happiness, drive us to selfishness and self-adulation, while at the same time hurting others, breaking familial peace, cutting-off relationships and other similar destructive behaviour. Never let it happen, as in the aforementioned story of Ibrāhīm ibn Adham, that we--the ones who have more wealth—are actually more 'needy' of money than the poor.

13

Towards a Life of Charity

ONCE, THE AMERICAN talk show host and philanthropist, Oprah Winfrey, gathered about a hundred people together to conduct a social experiment in which they were asked to set aside some of their vacation budget for charity. The savings were then given to those in need. A few months later, the same hundred were gathered together and asked whether there was any change in their lives. The answer they gave was yes, they felt that they had become happier after sharing with others.

***

Oprah's experiment was a smart way to encourage us to test ourselves. Indeed, giving donations or alms is one of the best tests because it is in direct opposition to selfishness, which is the source of all vices. To give is to prioritize the interest of others up and above our own.

It is said in the Qur'an that among the virtues that help us to develop piety (*al-birr*) is spending the wealth that we love.

> *Never will you attain to piety until you spend [in the way of Allah] from that which you love. And whatever you spend—indeed, Allah is aware of it.* (*Āl ʿImrān* 3: 92)

Testing ourselves by spending from the wealth that we love is in the same league as a trial from Allah, since spending our wealth for others is, in a worldly sense, making things difficult for us by making us relatively poorer.

> *And We will surely test you with something of fear and hunger and a loss of wealth and lives and fruits, but give good tidings to those who are patient, who, when disaster strikes them, say: 'Indeed we belong to Allah, and indeed to Him we will return.'* (*al-Baqarah* 2: 155-56)

The difference is that this test is subject to our control and not mandatory. Hence we have the option of not going through with it. This is why our tradition teaches that charity is a way of averting trials (*balāʾ*). That is, if we are willing to be charitable, in parting with the wealth that we love, then Allah would not necessarily send down His test—since we have accomplished it by creating *balāʾ* for ourselves and implemented His injunctions.

The neutralizing nature of the relationship between charity and divine trials is deeply rooted in the *sunnah* of Allāh (the Law of God).

How can we explain that alms prevent divine trials?

According to Islamic teachings, an event will take place if the requirements leading to the occurrence have been met. For example, the earth's gravitational pull will cause objects with mass to fall to the ground if dropped from above. A heavy rocket is able to rise in accordance with the principle of the conservation of momentum, which acts in opposition to gravity. The Laws of Allah apply not only in the empirical realm, but also in other realms called *'ālam al-amr*, the spiritual realm. Each of the realms has its own laws and is able to affect the other. The law of the empirical realm generates events, whereas the law of the spiritual realm operates against it. Thus, it is possible that empirical events do not happen as expected. And indeed, in addition to prayer and supplication, what is able to affect the law of *'ālam al-amr* is alms-giving.

Once, Prophet Muhammad (peace be upon him) was sitting with his Companions and a Jewish man passed by. Looking at him, the Prophet said: 'He will soon pass away.' A while later he passed them again, this time carrying a bundle of firewood. The Companions of the Prophet were rather surprised that, contrary to what the Prophet had predicted, he was still alive. The Prophet then called him over and asked him to put down the bundle of firewood and untie it. No sooner had he done that than a poisonous snake slipped out of the bundle.

The Prophet said: 'You were destined to die from a snakebite. You must have done something (to avert it).' The man replied: 'In the course of gathering wood I gave alms to a poor man who was in much difficulty.' The Prophet said: 'Alms-giving was what has saved you from being bitten fatally by the snake.'

Here exactly lies the problem of human beings. We lead lives obsessing over profit and loss or, more precisely, we are busy thinking how to maximize our profits, often by paying little or no attention to the living conditions of others who are worse off than us. We do not see people as they are, but we create our own perceptions of them. We envy people for the things they have which we do not. Our lives are filled with regret for what we could not achieve in the past, and with fears that in the future we will not achieve all that we aspire to. We also lose our perspective on the countless blessings we actually already have. This empties our life of spirituality and happiness. So if we want to be happy, let us learn from children, and maintain the innocence of the inner nature of the child in us.

Presumably, we do not need to wait to be 'forced' by Allah through adversity, before we feel the need to share or help others, just in order to get out of the trial. Instead, we need to continue to educate ourselves by testing ourselves, in the form of sharing and doing good unto others, whatever our situation.

Let us give our best and most loved possessions in charity. Giving is a mechanism to achieve meaning and blessings in our life. It paves the way to a life of happiness and saves us from the tests sent down by Allah. And it brings us closer to His love. Happy giving!

> *As for he who gives and fears Allah, and believes in the goodness [to come], We will ease him toward bliss.* (*al-Layl* 92: 5–7)

14

Turning Work into Passion

THREE MASONS WERE working side by side to build something. Someone asked one of them about what he was doing. He replied that he was building a wall. The second mason, responding to the same question, said that he was building a house, whereas the third one stated he was building a dwelling for a young family who would live in it, and he hoped that they would be comfortable and happy.

***

On the surface, the three masons are visibly working on the same task: laying bricks and other construction materials to build a structure. However, if we look at how they give meaning to what they do, we will see how different their attitudes towards their work are. The first one sees his work as nothing more than physical movements, which can also be replicated by animals or robots, while the second has awareness of his task being a creative one. Yet, the ultimate meaning was given by the third mason, since he deems his job as a manifestation of his love for others, his desire to build a comfortable and satisfying home for prospective occupants. So, we can easily predict which of the three bricklayers will deliver the maximum performance, both quantitatively and qualitatively.

Work is supposed to be a source of meaning in life. Moreover, a meaningful job will also give birth to a love and passion towards what one is doing. This in itself can be a source of happiness, without which work can only become a burden weighing us down every day. Setting love as the basis for our work will in turn propel us to do our utmost. As a result, whatever we are producing in our work will give rise to high quality products. At its peak, such meaningful work will not only become a source of happiness in the spiritual life but also a source of worldly success in this life.

The subsequent question is, what kind of work can be a source of positive meaning in life? The Qur'an teaches: 'Seek instead, by means of what God has granted you, [the good of] the life to come, without forgetting your own [rightful] share in this world.' (*al-Qaṣaṣ* 28: 77)

Through this verse, God explicitly and implicitly commands us to do our work as well as possible in order to seek His blessings, but the intent should not be restricted only to this worldly life, but also to the Afterlife. That is, to give a surplus of meaning to our activities. Aside from taking our fair allocation in this life, we must direct all our activities to the Hereafter. And, by attempting to fulfil the needs of the Hereafter, actually we are at the same time working to meet our spiritual needs—which, ultimately, are the source of our true happiness in this life.

Allah teaches us further on how we must regard our work:

> *[Indeed it is] they who follow God's revelation, and are constant in prayer, and spend on others, secretly and openly, out of what We provide for them as sustenance—it is they who may look forward to a bargain that can never fail (*tijārah lan tabūr*).* (*Fāṭir* 35: 29)

From this verse, we can conclude that God is willing to teach us about how we should give meaning to our work. Despite its function as a means to seek wealth, any type of work will only be meaningful provided it is based on a sound understanding of the essence of life, adorned with nuances of development and preservation of our spiritual relationship with God, and the spirit of philanthropy or good deeds.

Simply by relating all of our activities to our Lord, our work will actually be a source of positive meaning for our heart and soul. And only this way can our work become a source of our happiness.

Measuring the Levels of Worldly Love[1] —Al-Ghazālī

THIS WORLD IS a stage, or a market, visited by travellers on their way to somewhere else. Here they supply themselves with a range of provisions for the trip. Plainly, it is here that man, by using his bodily senses, gains some knowledge of the works of God and, through these works, of God himself. His view of Him will determine his future happiness. To acquire this knowledge, man's spirit descends into this realm of water and clay. As long as his senses are still intact, we say that he is still in 'this realm'. Otherwise, when all that remains are only his essential traits, it is said that he has gone to 'the other realm'.

Being in this world, man is in need of two things: first, protection and maintenance of the soul; second, care and maintenance of the body. Proper maintenance of man's soul, as indicated above, is achieved through knowledge and love of God. Once he is absorbed in love of anything

1. Al-Ghazali, *Meramu Kebahagiaan* (Jakarta: Penerbit Hikmah, 2002), p. 33.

other than God, he collapses. The body can be considered as a mere means of transport, and will vanish, while the soul lasts. The soul must take care of the body just as a pilgrim must take care of his camel on his way to Makkah; if he fails to do so his caravan will leave him and he will die in the desert.

The needs of the human body are simple, consisting only of three things: food, clothing and shelter. However, embedded in his body are bodily passions and desires that require satiating. They are inclined to rebel against his reason, which is only developed in the shadow of the desires, and they need to be restrained and controlled by the laws of God that are taught by prophets.

As to the world that we must deal with, we find it grouped into three sections: animals, plants and minerals. The products of all these three are constantly needed by man and have developed into three big industries–the work of the weavers, builders and metal workers. Once again, all of them have their own subsidiary branch; like tailors, masons and blacksmiths. Nothing can be completely independent of the other, which gives rise to a wide range of trading relations and often results in hatred, envy, jealousy and other spiritual diseases. As a consequence, quarrels and disputes take place, inciting the need for political and civil administration, as well as a legal system.

Thus, occupations and businesses in the world have become increasingly complicated, bringing about a sense of chaos. The major cause is that man has forgotten that his needs are actually only three–clothing, food and shelter–and that they exist only for the sake of making the body a viable vehicle for the soul on its way to the next world. They fall into the same mistake as the pilgrim heading for Makkah, who forgets about his destination and himself and finds himself busy feeding and decorating his camel. A person will necessarily be captivated and preoccupied by the world—which the Prophet reportedly said was more bewitching than Hārūt and Mārūt—unless he conducts the most rigorous control.

The deceitful character of this world can take several forms. First, it pretends that it will always stay with you while in fact it moves slowly away from you and bids farewell, as a shadow that seems to remain but in reality the reverse is the case. Similarly, the world presents itself in the guise of a beautiful woman, but she is immoral, pretending to love and care for you and then turning her back on you to devote herself to your enemy, leaving you to die out of disappointment and despair.

'Īsā saw the world unveiled in the form of an ugly old woman. He asked her how many husbands she had wedded. She replied that she had lost count. He enquired of her again whether they had died or had divorced her. She replied with the answer that she had killed them all. 'I wonder,' said 'Īsā, 'how could people fall into your spell after seeing what had happened to their predecessors?'

This old witch covered her face with an appealing veil, decked herself with gorgeous garments and valuable jewellery so that whoever cast an eye on her would fall in love with her instantly. Countless men followed her, ruining themselves. The Prophet Muhammad (peace be upon him) said that on the Day of Judgment, this world would appear in the form of a hideous hag. Her eyes would be green and she would have protruding teeth.

People would see her and exclaim: 'God forbid. Who is this ugly woman?' The angels would answer: 'This is the same world that you liked so much, for which you used to be jealous and quarrel with each other.' Then the witch would be thrown into Hell and she would ask: 'Where are my former lovers?' God, then, would command that the lovers also be thrown into it.

Anyone who wants to seriously reflect on the virtue of the past, the period when this universe was non-existent and the eternity of the future lay ahead, or the period when the world no longer exists, then he will find that life is a journey whose phases are reflected by years, by months, by miles a day and steps by the second. So, what words could describe a man's folly that he lives here as if he is going to live forever; that although he is not even sure of his next breath he plans for things for the next ten years to come, pondering about things that he may never need because he would very likely be buried underground by then.

After his death, overindulgence in the pleasures of this world would be like someone who has filled his stomach on selected and delicious food, then starts vomiting. Its deliciousness is gone, only to be substituted with unpleasantness. The more one indulges in the lusts of this world–gardens, carnal desires, gold, silver, etc.–the more bitterness he will feel when separated from it. He will feel a bitterness even more terrible than death because a soul that has made a habit of greed will continue to face suffering in the next world as a result of the pain of accumulated unsatisfied desires.

Another aspect of the dangerous nature of worldly things is that at first they seem trivial, but things that are considered trivial have branched out into innumerable pursuits, ready to consume all of one's time and energy. 'Īsā said: 'The seekers of this world are like a man who drinks sea water; the more he drinks the thirstier he becomes, and eventually he dies from an unquenchable thirst.' The Prophet Muhammad (peace be upon him) said: 'You cannot mingle in the world without being polluted by it, just as you cannot dive into the water without getting wet.'

The world is like a table spread for guests who come and go. There are abundant gold and silver plates of food and perfume. A sensible guest eats as much as he needs, inhales the fragrance then thanks the host and leaves. Whereas, a greedy guest tries to take some gold and silver plates with him that are wrenched from his hands, throwing him into a state of disappointment and embarrassment.

Let's recap on the description of the nature of this deceitful world with the following short parable: A group of people boarded a ship which would soon arrive at a beautiful island. The captain announced that the ship would stop for a few hours and the passengers would be allowed to take a short walk on the beach, but that afterwards they should re-board the ship quickly. When the ship stopped the passengers roamed in different directions. The first group took a short walk then came straight back, discovered that the ship was empty and chose the most comfortable places to wait.

The second group of passengers spent somewhat longer on the island, admiring the foliage and the trees and listening to the birds. Upon returning to the ship, they found the most comfortable places on the ship had been occupied, forcing them to settle for a slightly less comfortable position.

The third group walked further and found beautiful coloured stones which they brought back to the ship. Their tardiness left them sitting in the lowest part of the ship, where they found the rocks that they had brought—which had lost all their beauty—disturbed them.

The last group wandered too far and they could not hear the voice of the captain who called on them to immediately return to the ship, which finally sailed away without them. They loitered in a state of hopelessness and eventually died of starvation or fell prey to wild animals.

The first group reflects believers, who completely distance themselves from the world, and the last group are nonbelievers, who only take care of this world, ignoring what will come. The two groups in between are people who still have faith but keep themselves busy with, more or less, unsatisfactory worldly things.

Although we have said many things condemning the world, it must be kept in mind that there are some things in the world that are not included in it, such as knowledge and good deeds. One will bring with him the knowledge that he had to the world to come. His good deeds have passed but its effects remain by his side, especially through worship that has enabled him to constantly remember and love his God. Those are grouped in 'good deeds', which are revealed in the Qur'an as 'enduring good deeds'. (*al-Kahf* 18: 46)

There are good things in this world, such as marriage, food and clothing, which will be used sparingly by the sensible to help them attain happiness in the Hereafter.

Other objects, which captivate the mind and lure the faithful to love this world and ignore the next world, are in fact vile. They are mentioned by the Prophet in his saying: 'The world is accursed and everything contained within it is accursed, except the remembrance of Allah (*dhikr*) and everything that assists a person towards it.'

About the Author

HAIDAR BAGIR is an influential Islamic thinker based in Indonesia. He earned his master's degree from the Center for Middle Eastern Studies at Harvard University (1992), and a PhD in Philosophy from the University of Indonesia, with a year of research (2000–2001) at the Department of History and Philosophy of Science at Indiana University, Bloomington.

He has been the recipient of three Fulbright scholarships and his name has been included in the list of the 500 Most Influential Muslims by The Royal Islamic Strategic Studies Centre for several years in a row. Apart from his activities in various organizations and his being the director of Mizan, a publishing company, he has written a number of popular books. His latest book is *Learning to Live* from Rumi (2015).

He still actively gives religious lectures and teaches at a number of institutes. He is a sought after speaker at several scholarly seminars, especially in the fields of philosophy and contemporary Islamic thought.